PAPER
QUILLING
FOUR
SEASONS

PAPER QUILLING FOUR SEASONS

CHINESE STYLE

Zhu Liqun Paper Arts Museum

Better Link Press

On page 1
Fig. 1 *Four Seasons*
Dimensions: 39 by 54 centimeters
Using the change of color and other elements cleverly, the author depicts the sceneries of all seasons in one picture. The smaller, verdure loose coils represent newly sprung buds; the bigger, deep-green loose coils the luxuriant summer leaves; the yellow loose coils in triangle the falling yellow leaves in autumn that gather on the ground; and the light-blue loose coils the snowflakes dancing freely between trees. The whole work is ingeniously composed and brightly colored.

On pages 2 and 3
Fig. 2 *Autumn*
Dimensions: 54 by 39 centimeters
Autumn is the season of harvest. A whole year's hard work is now paid off with a bumper harvest, filling people's hearts with joy. This work presents the theme of autumn with red, orange and yellow colors. Red and orange represent the colors of maple leaves in autumn, and yellow the color of ripe grains. The three warm colors may best represent people's heart-felt joy.

For Zhu Liqun Paper Arts Museum
Project Designers: Yao Xiaoyan, Zhu Liqun
Text and Photographs: Wang Chenbo
Works: Yao Xiaoyan, Zhu Liqun, Liu Xiuxia, Qian Ciying, Wang Chenbo, Zhu Jiayan, Yan Wenjun, Chen Boyu, Qian Caidi, Tang Xiaoying, Ding Yijun, Li Liwen, Zhang Keqing, Zhang Danyi, Hu Weiyuan, Yang Ningyuan, Tang Shi, Tang Ge, Ji Yunting, Wu Xinyi, Shao Yunshan, Chen Longyun, Wang Enyue, Dai Yuming, Liu Boyuan, Qian Ruoyan, Tang Yiwen, Zhang Junping, Xu Minshu, Xu Huijue, Xue Suomei, Wang Minxiu
Technique Demonstration: Liu Xiuxia

Translation: Zhao Gang, Du Zhendong
Cover Design: Wang Wei
Interior Design: Li Jing, Hu Bin (Yuan Yinchang Design Studio)

Copy Editor: Gretchen Zampogna
Editors: Wu Yuezhou, Cao Yue
Editorial Director: Zhang Yicong
Senior Consultants: Sun Yong, Wu Ying, Yang Xinci
Managing Director and Publisher: Wang Youbu

ISBN: 978-1-60220-033-3

Address any comments about *Paper Quilling Four Seasons: Chinese Style* to:

Better Link Press
99 Park Ave
New York, NY 10016
USA

or

Shanghai Press and Publishing Development Co., Ltd.
F 7 Donghu Road, Shanghai, China (200031)
Email: comments_betterlinkpress@hotmail.com

Printed in China by Shenzhen Donnelley Printing Co., Ltd.

1   3   5   7   9   10   8   6   4   2

CONTENTS

Preface   *9*

Introduction   *13*

Chapter I   The Artistic Charm of Chinese-Style Paper Quilling   *17*
   1. Borrowing from Traditional Chinese Folk Custom Techniques   *18*
   2. Passing on the Characteristics of Traditional Chinese Painting   *18*
   3. Drawing Materials from Traditional Chinese Culture   *24*
   4. Possessing Unique Artistic Characteristics   *26*
   5. Embedding the Theme of the "24 Solar Terms"   *27*

Chapter II   Preparation   *29*
   1. Materials   *30*
   2. Tools   *31*
   3. Ten Techniques of Chinese-Style Paper Quilling   *34*
   4. Categories of Basic Elements of Chinese-Style Paper Quilling   *37*
      Lines and Scrolls   *37*
      Coils   *38*
      Loops   *39*
      Crescents   *40*

Chapter III   Beginner Tutorial   *43*
   1. Beginning of Spring   *44*
   2. Rain Water   *48*
   3. Waking of Insects   *51*
   4. Vernal Equinox   *54*
   5. Pure Brightness   *58*
   6. Grain Rain   *61*
   7. Beginning of Summer   *66*
   8. Grain Budding   *69*
   9. Grain in Ear   *72*
   10. Summer Solstice   *76*

CONTENTS

11. Slight Heat   *80*
12. Great Heat   *83*
13. Beginning of Autumn   *87*
14. Limit of Heat   *90*
15. White Dew   *93*
16. Autumnal Equinox   *97*
17. Cold Dew   *100*
18. Frost's Descent   *104*
19. Beginning of Winter   *109*
20. Lesser Snow   *112*
21. Great Snow   *117*
22. Winter Solstice   *121*
23. Slight Cold   *125*
24. Great Cold   *129*

Chapter IV   Intermediate Tutorial   *133*

1. Spring in the Air   *134*
2. Verdant Mountains and Blue Water   *140*
3. Blossoming Moth Orchids   *144*
4. Swan on Water   *148*
5. A Fine Autumn Day   *152*
6. Flower Petals Falling in Profusion   *157*
7. Fruits of All Seasons   *161*
8. Flowers of All Seasons   *165*

Chapter V   Advanced Tutorial   *173*

1. Spring Mountains   *174*
2. Summer Water   *180*
3. Autumn Forest   *186*
4. Winter Snow   *192*

On page 5
Fig. 3   *Flower in a Vase*
Dimensions: 15 by 15 centimeters
This work, though small and concise, is rich in connotation, carrying many auspicious meanings in traditional Chinese culture. The vase and flower together symbolizes peace in all seasons, the fish on the vase, getting more than you wish for, and the shape of *ruyi*-scepter in the vase, complete satisfaction. In addition, the vase is similar to the Chinese blue-and-white porcelain in color, which, placed on a brown table, looks full of ancient charm.

On facing page
Fig. 4   Paper scrolls.

Above
Fig. 5   Paper strips.

PREFACE

Many lovers of the art of paper quilling ask us a very interesting question: How can I learn this art better and faster? I'm not sure whether this question can be asked of other forms of art, but you can indeed learn paper quilling faster and better, so long as you are a keen observer and a bold explorer, and love thinking and change.

Faced with the zigzag components of a colorful paper quilling work, beginners may either find it too difficult to learn, or become fascinated with it, if they understand by observation and analysis that the secret of paper quilling lies in the varied combinations of various simple elements. This is the difference between low-level learning based on initial visual observation and in-depth learning that brings into play the "anatomical" function of visual observation. An observant learner always learns on his or her own initiative, and that is why they can learn faster and better.

Some learners are cautious followers. They follow book instructions closely, trembling at every stage for fear of making a mistake. Consequently, they are often unsatisfied with themselves and consider paper quilling hard to learn. Other learners are bold and are always ready to explore this art themselves. They do not care about making mistakes, regarding mistakes as a way to learn through comparison with the "correct" method. They are certainly faster and better learners.

In addition, observant and explorative learners are often good thinkers and good at learning through comparison. They may compare their own work with book examples to find similarities and differences. They may also compare different examples, different elements and even their own different making processes, from which they can detect directions of learning with great sensitivity. In their eyes, skills are not their masters but their servants. "Practice makes perfect" does not simply mean diligence, but more

On facing page
Fig. 6 *The Spring Girl*
Dimensions: 39 by 54 centimeters
Chinese people often compare spring to a young girl who travels across the vast land of China to knock open the door of iced rivers, awaken animals from hibernation and dye the twigs and buds green. This work outlines a plump and beautiful spring girl with white lines. The green leaves surrounding her give viewers a keen sense of spring.

importantly refers to the active learning spirit. The value of skills lies in their application. For a blind copier, even if he has succeeded in making the most exquisite raindrop flower petal, it can only be used on one flower. However, after careful observation and comparison, he may find much larger space for the raindrop element. For an artist rich in imagination, this element can be used almost everywhere. Therefore, our suggestion is to be a bold explorer and a good thinker at once.

It satisfies some learners to duplicate book examples successfully. However, the joy of paper quilling does not stop here. Creation—creation alone—is the real joy in the learning process. Do not stop at simple imitation. Take a step forward, and you will be able to experience your potential for creation.

The works included in this book demonstrate the 24 solar terms in a year. They are created by the most ordinary learners in our Paper Arts Museum. Though most of them started to learn paper quilling not long ago, they are full of inspirations and good at the creative use of different paper quilling elements. They do not fear failure and are bold enough to use what they hear and see in daily life in their artistic creation. When told their works were to be compiled into a book so that more lovers of the paper quilling art can benefit, they all said, "This is the real joy we obtain from learning paper quilling."

Zhu Liqun

Fig. 8 *Bees and Flowers*
Dimensions: 15 by 15 centimeters
The purple petals, yellow stamens and green leaves work together to form a full-blown flower. The bees are hovering around the flower, as if attracted by its dim fragrance.

On facing page
Fig. 7 *Summer*
Dimensions: 39 by 54 centimeters
Summer is a season brimming with life. This work presents the luxuriant vegetation of summer with different shades of green, the vitality of life with abundant naturally curved lines, and the season's exuberant leaves with green paper scrolls. The picture shows a vigorous green summer.

INTRODUCTION

*P*aper quilling is a form of art that uses long, colorful paper slips as the basic materials for creating basic elements of diversified forms with the help of hands and some simple tools. These elements are then put together or superimposed to produce works of art. Due to the simple materials it uses and the diverse forms and beautiful shapes it takes, paper quilling has become popular with an increasing number of people, both old and young.

The art of paper quilling has a long history. It developed into a relatively mature handwork in Europe as early as the Middle Ages. Today, it has become an independent art form. Although paper quilling is still less known today, it integrates the artistic characteristics of painting and sculpture perfectly, rendering the works more forms of representation and more artistic styles with various techniques based on the elasticity, flexibility and plasticity of paper. With paper quilling, you are capable of unlimited expression, either realistic or abstract, wild or aesthetic, rough or refined.

Along with the more and more in-depth Sino-Western exchanges, paper quilling, an art form originated in the West, has also entered China, attracting many followers with its elegance and antiquity. Among them, Zhu Liqun took the lead to establish the first paper-quilling workshop in China, which has now developed into a paper-quilling museum. With his guidance, lovers of this art form have integrated traditional Chinese culture and artistic expressions into traditional Western paper quilling, producing works with unique Chinese characteristics. In his museum, paper quilling is taught as a rudimentary form of art that can enable learners, young and old, to learn by analogy. Gradually, they will form their own understanding of this artistic form through hands-on practice.

On facing page
Fig. 9 *An Autumn Day*
Dimensions: 39 by 54 centimeters
Maple leaves turn red when autumn comes. This work focuses on likeness in spirit. It uses red and purple curved lines to imitate the maple trunk and red loose coils to represent falling maple leaves, creating a sense of autumn with maple leaves gradually becoming red and then falling. The whole picture shows the theme that all things on Earth will decline when they pass their zeniths.

Paper quilling is very easy to learn in the beginning, requiring nothing more than a roll of paper, a pair of scissors and a bottle of glue. Compared with traditional Western paper quilling, the Chinese-style paper quilling is even more user-friendly to beginners. We use the simplest and most fundamental techniques to produce infinite patterns and shapes, which can be mastered even by those who know nothing about this art. All they need to understand the charm of this artistic form is patience and creativity.

This book is a follow-up to *Paper Quilling: Chinese Style*, the first work on paper quilling produced by Zhu Liqun and other members of the museum. Based on sceneries in the four seasons, it displays the making of each item with full-color pictures in three tutorials, elementary, intermediate and advanced. The elementary tutorial focuses on exhibiting the content of the 24 Chinese solar terms with simple elements in concise composition. The intermediate tutorial is richer in elements and theme, with diversified colors showing the characteristics and changes of the four seasons to the fullest. The advanced tutorial is characterized by bigger pictures with more complicated and fuller compositions. You can choose to start from the easiest to the most difficult or directly challenge the advanced tutorial to gain a higher sense of achievement.

Fig. 10 *Flowers and Leaves*
Dimensions: 27 by 27 centimeters
This work uses different elements to present various kinds of flowers and leaves. It offers reference to flower and leaf presentation in paper quilling.

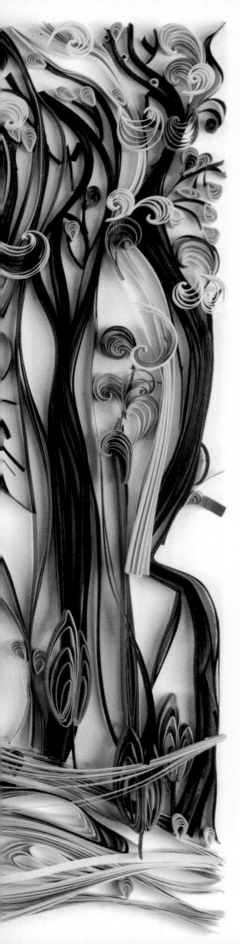

CHAPTER I

The Artistic Charm of Chinese-Style Paper Quilling

Compared with traditional Western paper quilling, the Chinese-style paper quilling is rather distinctive, as it has given birth to many novel techniques of creation and borrowed wisdom from the traditional profound cultural essence ranging from folk arts, paintings, myths, poetries, auspicious symbols, idoms to time-honored solar terms which are still used today. In this sense, it is an art form that integrates tradition and innovation.

Fig. 11 *Scenery*
Dimensions: 27 by 27 centimeters
Using smooth lines, rich patterns and diversified colors, the author presents a beautiful scene common in rural China by depicting trees, farmland and animal. The old yellow ox in the distance adds vitality to the picture and reflects the harmonious beauty of nature.

1. Borrowing from Traditional Chinese Folk Custom Techniques

Traditional Chinese culture is extensive and profound. The techniques of wood carving, jade carving and paper cutting are all fine embodiment of the wisdom of ancient Chinese. From wood carving, we borrow the technique of displaying three-dimensional contouring on a plane surface; from jade carving, the unique mellow and full lines; and from paper cutting, the alteration between *yin* and *yang*, two opposite yet complementary energies. These borrowings have rendered Chinese-style paper quilling extremely strong and rich in artistic expression (fig. 12).

2. Passing on the Characteristics of Traditional Chinese Painting

Known for its unique lines, perspectives, themes and connotations, Chinese painting is a major category of painting with a long history. In Chinese-style paper quilling works, the artistic technique similar to blank-leaving in Chinese painting has been used extensively, and the composition featuring the interrelations between emptiness and substantiality has also appeared in high frequency, offering the works an appealing energy (fig. 13 and see fig. 15 on page 20).

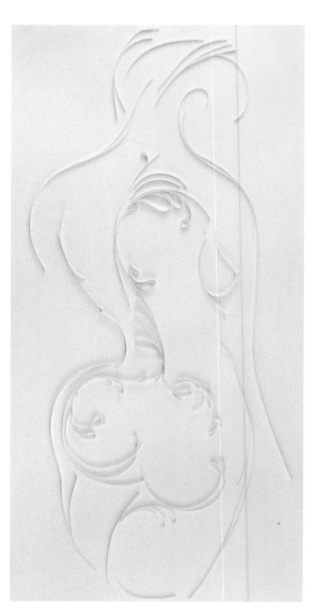

Fig. 12 *Human Body*
Dimensions: 90 by 45 centimeters
The artist has a precise understanding of the muscular lines of a human body. Using natural and smooth curved lines, he/she outlines the back of a plump woman with great felicity. In addition, he/she makes the best use of shadows to display the beauty of the human body.

On facing page
Fig. 13 *Mountains and Rivers*
Dimensions: 30 by 45 centimeters
Like Chinese painting, many works of Chinese-style paper quilling present mountains and rivers. In this work, the author links mountain peaks with zigzag rivers and leaves a lot of blank space, as well. The work is ingenious in composition and appropriate in density. Even though the elements used are simple, they work together to give viewers a feeling of momentum.

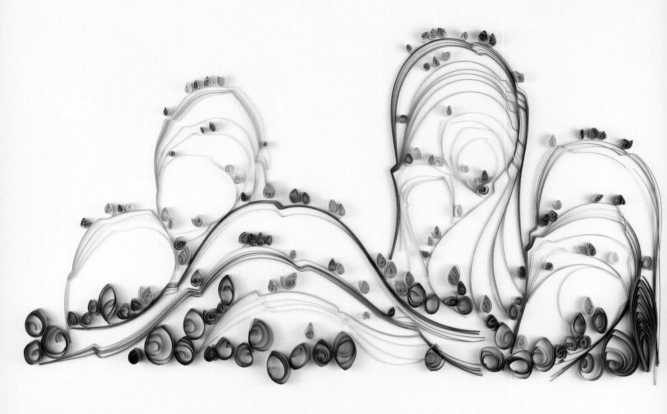

Fig. 14 *Spring Mountains*
Dimensions: 54 by 39 centimeters
Spring is the time for all things on earth to wake up. The spring shower and wind turn mountains and lakes into a world of lovely green. In this work, the author has borrowed from the techniques of traditional Chinese landscape painting, imitating the undulation of mountains with paper slips. Each slip has a carefully designed pattern, which gives full play to the plasticity, flexibility, and changeability of this basic element. The streamlined paper slips with the same color but different color gradations collaborate to create a magnificent scene of undulating mountains.

Fig. 15 *Bird on Flowers*
Dimensions: 39 by 39 centimeters
Birds-and-flower painting is a major category in traditional Chinese painting. The author depicts a bird perching on a flower branch with thick ink and light colors. The work, borrowing both fine brushwork techniques and freehand brushwork techniques from traditional Chinese painting, looks vivid and lifelike.

Fig. 16 *Flowers and Grass*
Dimensions: 27 by 27 centimeters
Different from most works of Chinese-style paper quilling, this work uses the method of filling to make flower petals and leaves, a reflection of the author's unique style of creation.

Varied in form: In terms of size and form, Chinese paintings consist of vertically-hung scrolls, sketches, scrolls, fans, long scrolls, etc., all of which we have borrowed for Chinese-style paper quilling. For example, all the works representing the 24 solar terms are in the form of sketches, with round or square compositions. In the intermediate tutorial, we have borrowed the form of vertically-hung scrolls. In addition, the large vertically-hung scroll and long scroll are also frequently used in our works (see figs. 12–13 on pages 18–19).

Beautiful in artistic mood: Chinese paper quilling requires not only vivid images, but also beauty in artistic mood. Like Chinese painting, it focuses on "likeness in spirit," rather than "likeness in form," pursuing a kind of beauty between "likeness and unlikeness." The images it depicts are more changeable, causing endless imaginings (fig. 16).

Free in composition: In traditional Western paper quilling, it is often the case that the image is filled up with different elements. However, since Chinese-style paper quilling borrows from Chinese painting the mode of composition that balances the picture by leaving blank space and focusing on contrasts between emptiness and substantiality, it enjoys more flexibility and freedom in composition (fig. 14).

Fig. 17 *Dancing Cranes*
Dimensions: 54 by 39 centimeters
The crane always keeps the company of immortals in traditional Chinese culture, symbolizing auspiciousness, longevity and elegance. In this work, the author cleverly uses various elements in Chinese paper quilling to depict two lifelike white cranes. The curved sky-blue lines look like white snow in winter, and the cranes are dancing in white, vivid and beautiful.

Fig. 18 *Orchids*
Dimensions: 27 by 27 centimeters
In traditional Chinese culture, the orchid is regarded as symbolizing elegance and grace, and it is known as "gentleman of flowers." The author presents the features of orchids in spring with purple, pink and white colors.

3. Drawing Materials from Traditional Chinese Culture

Chinese-style paper quilling features the rich connotations of traditional Chinese culture from different perspectives and uses them to display the culture's diversity.

Fairytales: In the long course of historical development, the Chinese people have created numerous fairytales that are still popular today. These fairytales, which reflect the relationship between man and nature and different social formations, have a far-reaching impact on the literature and art of later generations. Chinese-style paper quilling can vividly duplicate the characters and scenes of ancient Chinese fairytales with a rich variety of representational methods.

Poetry: Poetry is the essence of traditional Chinese literature. Different literary genres assumed different historical statuses in different Chinese dynasties. Of all the literary genres, the most famous ones are Tang poetry, Song

Fig. 19 *Radiant with Joy*
Dimensions: 39 by 39 centimeters
The magpie symbolizes auspiciousness and happiness in traditional Chinese culture. When a magpie perches on a plum branch, it means "radiant with joy." The color scheme in this work is rather unique. The black magpie and the bright-colored plum flowers offer viewers a sense of auspiciousness and joy.

poems and Yuan dramas. Chinese-style paper quilling, which borrows from the forms of expression from traditional Chinese painting, enjoys an innate advantage in presenting poetry.

Auspicious moral: The Chinese culture of auspiciousness, which expresses people's wish for a beautiful life, has gradually grown into a complete system in its long course of development. Chinese paper quilling works reference auspicious images in traditional Chinese culture to express good wishes, such as the *ruyi*-scepter, the crane and the magpie (figs. 17–19).

Stories of idioms: Chinese idiom is a unique characteristic of traditional Chinese culture. They are fixed in structure, often with four characters, concise in expression and profound in meaning. In Chinese-style paper quilling, the artists often try to vividly present the stories behind idioms with paper slips.

In addition, the artists have also attempted to present other forms of traditional Chinese culture, such as the 24 solar terms in this book. They combine art and life to instill rich connotations into their works.

Fig. 20 *Autumn Leaves*
Dimensions: 120 by 60 centimeters
This work presents the theme of autumn leaves covering the ground in an abstract way. Numerous brown and yellow leaves are used to artistically create the atmosphere of a golden autumn, outstanding in artistic expressive force.

4. Possessing Unique Artistic Characteristics

Having integrated traditional Chinese culture and many forms of representation in traditional Chinese art, Chinese-style paper quilling has developed its own unique characteristics.

A rich variety of elements: Instead of trying mechanically to maintain the systematic arrangement elements, Chinese-style paper quilling gives top priority to the work itself, as the elements are considered to serve the work, not vice versa. In this book, many elements are created by the artists themselves, and uniquely enhance the works' power of expression.

Flexible creation techniques: Compared with the technique of assembling by pasting popular elements in traditional Western paper quilling, the techniques used in Chinese-style paper quilling are more flexible. These include outlining with a single line, arranging multiple lines, changing the form of elements, superimposing the elements hierarchically, and even scattering the elements randomly (fig. 20).

Bold color schemes: Since it does not sedulously pursue likeness in form, Chinese-style paper quilling is bolder and freer in using colors. Learners can disregard the restriction of the original colors of the elements and create a color scheme of their own, so long as the overall work looks harmonious and beautiful in color.

Freedom, variation and flexibility are the most important characteristics of Chinese-style paper quilling that we have emphasized all along in the teaching process. After reading this book, we believe our readers can also give full play to their imaginations and create unique works.

5. Embedding the Theme of the "24 Solar Terms"

A solar term is any of the 24 points in traditional Chinese lunar calendar that matches a particular astronomical event or signifies some natural phenomenon. The points are spaced 15 degrees apart along the ecliptic and are used by lunisolar calendars to stay synchronized with the seasons. Having been used for more than 2,000 years, the 24 solar terms were officially listed as a representative work of human non-substantial cultural heritage of UNESCO on Nov. 30, 2016.

As early as the Spring and Autumn and the Warring States Period (770–221 BC), Chinese people had discovered the rule of movement of the sun between the Tropic of Capricorn and the Tropic of Cancer. Eight solar terms were mentioned in "Twelve Months" of the *Spring and Autumn Annals of Lord Lu Buwei*, a book compiled in the late Warring States Period. They were Beginning of Spring, Vernal Equinox, Beginning of Summer, Summer Solstice, Beginning of Autumn, Autumnal Equinox, Beginning of Winter and Winter Solstice. These eight solar terms are considered the most important of all the 24 solar terms, for they accurately mark the change of seasons, thus serving as clear divisions of a year. In 104 BC, the 24 solar terms were included into *Taichu Calendar*, the first relatively complete calendar in China.

The 24 solar terms reflect changes in the four seasons and in temperature, climate and phenology; nature presents different sceneries in each solar term. Drawing upon the different characteristics of each solar term, this book attempts to reflect the seasonal changes, however slight they might be, in sketches and larger works.

Table of the 24 Solar Terms

Seasons	Months	Solar Terms	
Spring	1st month	Beginning of Spring	Rain Water
	2nd month	Waking of Insects	Vernal Equinox
	3rd month	Pure Brightness	Grain Rain
Summer	4th month	Beginning of Summer	Grain Budding
	5th month	Grain in Ear	Summer Solstice
	6th month	Slight Heat	Great Heat
Autumn	7th month	Beginning of Autumn	Limit of Heat
	8th month	White Dew	Autumnal Equinox
	9th month	Cold Dew	Frost's Descent
Winter	10th month	Beginning of Winter	Lesser Snow
	11th month	Great Snow	Winter Solstice
	12th month	Slight Cold	Great Cold

CHAPTER II
Preparation

*T*his chapter introduces the preparatory work for creating a paper quilling piece, including the materials, tools, techniques and basic elements. Paper is the carrier of the paper quilling art and the most important material. And the quality, color and width of the paper slips are key to a work's success. Although paper quilling does not rely on specific tools for creation, we can still use some simple tools to achieve maximum results with little effort. "The 10 techniques of Chinese-style paper quilling," which are based on our own paper quilling experience, can help readers grasp this art as quickly as possible. The introduction of the basic elements will enable them to learn the making of the basic elements systematically, as well as these elements' variations.

Fig. 21 *Peach Flower Grove*
Dimensions: 50 by 50 centimeters
The whole work consists of many red curved lines that outline a large grove of peach flowers. The pink flowers are dotted here and there to enhance the visual impact.

Fig. 22 Paper scrolls.

1. Materials

With the popularization of the paper quilling art, people can buy paper slips specifically designed for paper quilling from stores more conveniently. Of course, they can also choose the paper they like and cut it into slips. It's important to choose paper that is flexible, elastic and appropriately thick; otherwise, it may reduce the power of artistic expression of the work.

Different works require paper slips of different widths. Most of the works in this book use paper slips 5 millimeters wide, which are adequate for most Chinese-style paper quilling works. In addition, some works use paper slips 1.5 and 3 millimeters wide to make smaller elements and present details. In larger works, we may choose paper slips 1 centimeter wide or even thicker to match a work's size and give it momentum.

Chinese-style paper quilling does not have a specific requirement for background paper. People can make their own choice based on their own preferences. Most of the works in this book use white watercolor paper and embossed paper of different colors.

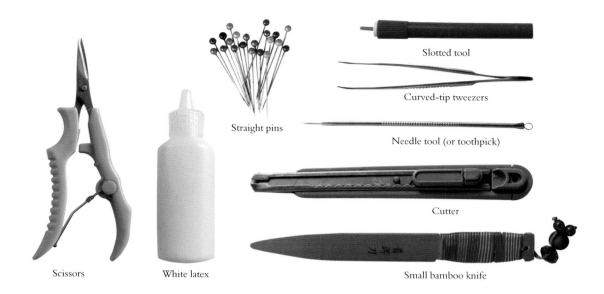

Slotted tool

Curved-tip tweezers

Straight pins

Needle tool (or toothpick)

Cutter

Scissors

White latex

Small bamboo knife

2. Tools

Chinese-style paper quilling requires simple tools. Apart from those we introduce here, learners can also give full play to their imaginations and discover tools in everyday life to help creation.

Slotted tool: This is the most common tool in traditional Western paper quilling, used specifically to roll paper slips. You can simply put the paper slip into the slot on its front end and then roll it. In addition, you can also use the thicker tail end for this purpose.

Small bamboo knife: The knife used frequently in this book is actually a tea knife that was originally used to loosen the Pu'er tea cake. Small, light and safe, it is ideal for stroking and scraping paper slips. You can also find a similar tool at home for this purpose.

Straight pins: These are used to stabilize paper slips and other elements at the initial stage of production. They are not needed at all after you have familiarized yourself with the techniques of Chinese-style paper quilling.

White latex: This is used to paste the paper slips and elements onto the background.

Curved-tip tweezers: These are used to pick up, arrange and fix smaller elements accurately.

Needle tool (or toothpick): This is used to dip white latex and apply it accurately onto the paper slips to make the work cleaner.

Scissors: These are used to trim the redundant part of a paper slip.

Cutter: This is for cutting paper and paper slips.

You can either use the above tools or other tools. After you are familiar with the techniques, you can try to use fewer tools and more of your hands for creation. In addition, in Chinese-style paper quilling, we do not advocate the use of paper templates. They can indeed make the production of elements easier, but at the same time they reduce the possibility of a freer and more flexible work.

Fig. 23 *A Summer Day*
Dimensions: 54 by 39 centimeters
Summer is the season when grapes become ripe. The author imitates grapevines with many blue crescents and strings of grapes with purple loose coils. The whole work is elegant and graceful, making viewers feel cool in the scorching summer.

3. Ten Techniques of Chinese-Style Paper Quilling

The 10 techniques are based on our experience of many years. Learners can take them as the starting point and explore unique techniques themselves. An excellent paper quilling work often results from creativity and imagination.

Smoothing: Hold one end of a paper slip with the thumb and forefinger of your left hand, and put a small bamboo knife against the back side of the paper slip with your right hand. Put your right thumb on the front side of the paper slip and stroke the paper slip from head to tail. This can produce gently curved lines on the paper slip and increase its plasticity.

You may also not use the knife, but stroke the paper slip with your forefinger and thumb several times to achieve the same effect.

Scraping: This is basically the same as smoothing. If you use a small bamboo knife, then you need to press your thumb on the other side of the paper slip against the knife more closely. If the knife is not used, then you need to stroke with your thumb and forefinger more forcibly. This will produce strong and natural curves on the paper slip.

There are two differences between scraping and smoothing. First, the force applied is different. Second, smoothing is done in the initial stage for preparation, while scraping can be directly used to shape the paper slip.

Bending: Bend the paper slip into any curved lines with both of your hands for shaping.

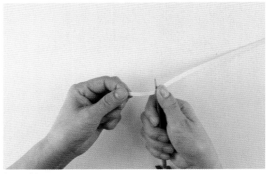

Smoothing

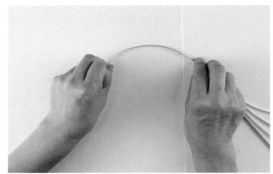

Bending

Scraping

Scrolling

Pulling

Pasting

Scrolling: Make the paper slip into a roll with a slotted tool or a cylinder. After familiarizing yourself with the technique, you can simply roll the paper slip with your fingers.

Pulling: Paste the beginning ends of several paper slips together, hold the middle sections of the slips loosely with one hand, and pull out different lengths with another hand until they form the shape you want.

Pinching

Pasting: White latex is needed to paste the treated paper slips together for basic elements and to fix the basic elements onto the background. The amount of white latex used and the technique of pasting determine the beauty of the basic elements, while whether the elements are pasted in the right places determines the overall effect of the work.

Pinching: After the paper slips are made into basic elements, use your thumb and forefinger to pinch them to produce some sharp angles. This can enrich the shapes of the basic elements.

Pressing

Pressing: Press the paper slips into different shapes you need with your thumb and forefinger.

Stacking: Stack multiple basic elements to create the second or even the third layer to make the picture more hierarchical and three-dimensional.

Stacking

Adjusting: Adjust the basic elements, lines, shapes and composition of the work to meet the artist's requirement.

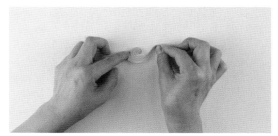
Adjusting

Fig. 24 *Waiting*
Dimensions: 39 by 54 centimeters
Beneath a luxuriant tree stands a girl looking into the distance. Is she waiting for her loved one to return from afar, or expecting the coming of destiny? Using various elements, the author has ingeniously created a girl in waiting.

4. Categories of Basic Elements of Chinese-Style Paper Quilling

Chinese-style paper quilling is free and flexible, which means that its elements also enjoy more freedom and variety. We classify the elements in this book into four categories, which, encompassing various techniques, constitute all our works. Each category consists of one basic element and its variations. Based on the four categories, the various elements made of paper slips, and the unique color schemes, you can often produce works of unparalleled beauty.

Lines and Scrolls

In Chinese-style paper quilling, lines are not only the original state of paper slips, but also one of the most fundamental elements in paper quilling works. Scrolls are the spiral curved lines produced by releasing a paper slip from a slotted tool. Simple as they are, the two elements can produce unexpected visual effects if used flexibly. In this book, you will see many works that reflect the authors' superb use of the two most basic elements for composition.

Straight line

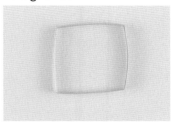

Straight line is the original state of a paper slip.

Curved line

These are formed by scraping straight lines and making them bend naturally.

Broken line

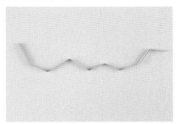

This is formed by pinching angles out of a straight line.

Zigzag line

This is the broken line with zigzags.

Basic scroll

Roll the paper slip with a slotted tool and then release it to form a basic scroll.

Long-tail scroll

When rolling a paper slip with a slotted tool, you can leave a relatively large section of the paper slip unrolled, thus producing a long-tail scroll.

Coils

In Western paper quilling, most of the elements are based on loose coils, which can be changed into various other shapes through pinching and pressing. Elements in this category are generally known as coils.

Basic coil

1 Take out a paper slip, roll up its beginning end with a slotted tool, and then release it.

2 Cut the redundant part and paste the tail end with white latex.

3 A loose coil is thus complete.

Tight coil

This is formed when the paper slip is rolled up more tightly.

Ring coil

This is a hollow coil with the external part tightly rolled up, resembling a ring.

Teardrop coil

This is formed by pinching one end of a loose coil into a sharp angle.

Curved teardrop coil

Bend the angle of a teardrop coil to form a curved teardrop coil.

Marquise coil

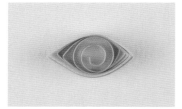

Pinch both ends of a loose coil into sharp angles to form a marquis coil.

Curved marquise coil

This is formed by bending the two sharp angles of a marquise coil in opposite directions.

Bamboo-leaf coil

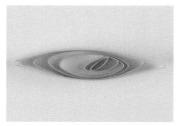

Pinch the middle part of a marquise coil flat to form a bamboo-leaf coil.

Quadrangular coil

Pinch a loose coil and make four angles to form a quadrangular coil.

Half-circle coil

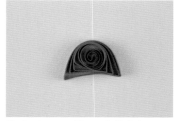

Pinch a loose coil into a half circle to form a half-circle coil.

Triangular coil

Pinch a loose coil and produce a triangle to form a triangular coil.

Tower coil

Produce a long and slim isosceles triangle following the method of making a triangular coil. Slightly indent the hemlines inward to form a tower coil.

Loops

A loop is made by pasting the beginning and tail ends of one or more bent paper slips together. Plump in shape, smooth in expression and rich in variation, it is often used as a structural element.

Basic loop

1 Stack several paper slips and paste their beginning ends together.

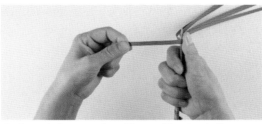

2 Smooth the paper slips with a small bamboo knife.

3 Bend the paper slips into a loop and pull them downward into different lengths and hierarchies.

4 Cut the redundant part and paste the beginning and tail ends together with white latex to complete a basic loop.

Raindrop loop

Adjust a basic loop and make it into a plump raindrop loop.

Oval loop

Paste the exterior side of the beginning end of the paper slip and the interior side of the tail end together. Adjust the shape to get an oval loop.

Leaf loop

Pinch one end of a basic loop into a sharp angle to form a leaf loop.

Half-circle loop

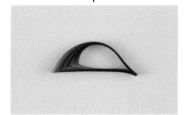

Pinch a basic loop into a half circle to form a half-circle loop.

Heart-shaped loop

Make a basic loop into a heart-shaped loop using the techniques of pressing, pinching, pasting and adjusting.

Crescents

The crescent is an element unique of Chinese-style paper quilling. In addition, many other forms of crescents have been developed based on the basic crescent using multiple techniques. The crescent is flexible in composition and use and its lines are in good order but not monotonous. Crescents can be used either as an outline or as fillers. They can also be used as supplementary elements to integrate into the work or constitute a complete work all by themselves. The use of crescent elements is a major characteristic of Chinese-style paper quilling.

Basic crescent

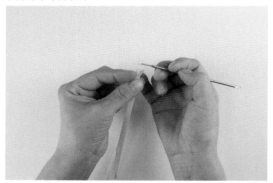

1 Take out several paper slips and paste their beginning ends together.

2 Smooth the slips with a small bamboo knife.

3 Hold the middle part of the paper slip with one hand and pull out different lengths from the tail end with another hand.

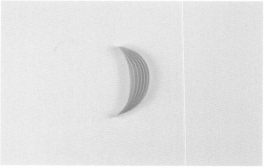

4 Paste the place you held and cut the redundant part of the paper slips to complete a basic crescent.

Wave crescent

In making a wave crescent, you can roll up the beginning end of the paper slips with a slotted tool so that the slip bends dramatically inward. Thus is completed a wave crescent.

Ruyi scepter-shaped crescent

Pinch the wavy end of a wave crescent to form a *ruyi* scepter-shaped crescent.

Harp crescent

Scrape one end or both ends of a basic crescent with a small bamboo knife toward the opposite direction to form a harp crescent.

Cicada-wing crescent

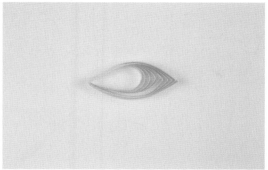

Spiral crescent

Roll up the tail end of a wave crescent in the opposite direction dramatically to form a spiral crescent.

S crescent

Make a long and slim basic crescent and scrape an arc in the opposite direction out of its tail end with a small bamboo knife to form an S crescent.

Raindrop crescent

Bend the tail of a basic crescent in the opposite direction and paste it together with the beginning end to form a raindrop crescent.

Paste the beginning and tail ends of a basic crescent and then pinch the middle of the crescent to form a sharp angle. Thus is completed a cicada-wing crescent.

CHAPTER III
Beginner Tutorial

*T*he 24 works in this chapter integrate the 24 solar terms typical of China. They are simple in structure, but rich in connotation, vivid and interesting. Through practicing with these works, you will be able to make a comprehensive use of the tools, materials, techniques, methods and basic elements we introduce in the previous chapters. You can also have hands-on experience of color collocation and picture composition, thus increasing your understanding of and interest in paper quilling. Now, please join us to explore the colorful kingdom of Chinese-style paper quilling.

Fig. 25 *Flowers and Grass*
Dimensions: 27 by 27 centimeters
This work is untraditional in shape and surrealistic in style.

43

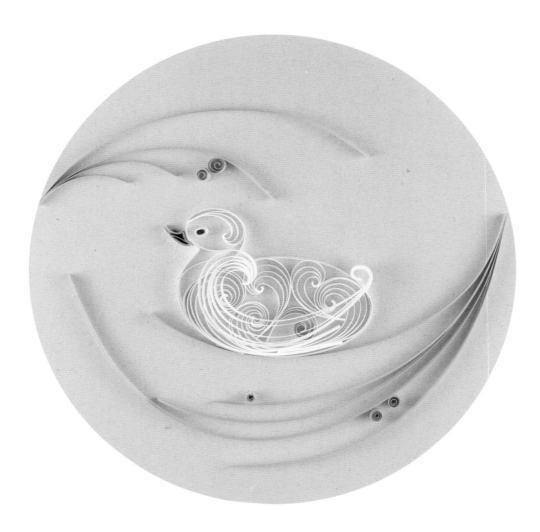

1. Beginning of Spring

Beginning of Spring (*lichun*) normally falls on Feb. 3 to 5 each year. It is the first of the 24 solar terms and an important one in Chinese tradition. By then, the east wind brings warm air, melting the ice and snow and revitalizing things on earth. During these days in ancient times, the emperor would greet the coming of spring with his officials and officers and pray for a bumper harvest. The ordinary people would prefer to celebrate this solar term by traveling, exchanging gifts, planting winter jasmines, setting up spring banners and eating spring rolls.

This work attempts to reproduce the picturesque scene created by the great Chinese poet Su Shi (1037–1101) in his poetic lines: Beyond the bamboo grove, several peach trees are in bloom. The river is warming up, which the ducks are the first to feel. In the work is a yellow duckling swimming in the water among some peach branches. The gentle spring wind creates ripples and brings warmth.

Materials and Elements

Duckling: ◯ loop: oval loop; line: curved line

Feathers and wing: ◯ ◯ crescent: wave crescent

Duckling eye: ● ◯ coil: tight coil

Duckling beak: ◓ coil: tower coil

Peach branches: ◯ line: curved line

Peach leaves: ● coil: loose coil

Background: white watercolor paper (suggested size: 27 by 27 centimeters), blue-gray embossed paper (suggested size: a piece of round paper with a diameter of 21 centimeters)

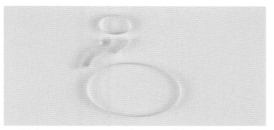

1 Make two oval loops, one bigger and the other smaller, with the lemon-yellow paper slips. The smaller one serves as the head of the duckling and the bigger one its body. Then make three curved lines following the picture to serve as the neck.

2 Paste five white paper slips on the beginning end, and then scrape the paper with a small bamboo knife or a similar tool until it curves.

3 Roll the paper from the beginning end with the slotted tool, adding more curvature to it.

4 Hold the paper near the beginning end with one hand, and use another hand to draw the paper slips downward with different lengths, so the curvature of the slips proportionately increases from inside out.

5 Paste the end together with white latex, and then cut the redundant part to complete the wave crescent, which is a variation of the basic crescent and a very common element in Chinese-style paper quilling.

6 Make six wave crescents of different sizes and layers with white paper slips.

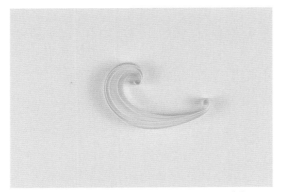

7 Make a wave crescent with two lemon-yellow and three white paper slips, with the lemon-yellow slips as the outermost layers and the white slips as the internal layers. Roll the end of the wave crescent with the slotted tool to make it curve. This will serve as the wing of the duckling.

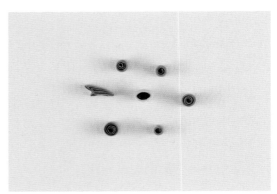

8 Make an oval tight coil with black and yellow paper slips, which will serve as the eye of the duckling. Make a loose coil with the orange-red paper slip and then pinch and produce a tower coil out of it as the duckling's mouth. Make several loose coils with grass-green paper slips, which will serve as peach leaves.

9 Make nine light-blue curved lines for peach branches by scraping.

10 Stick the blue-gray circular embossed paper onto the center of the white watercolor paper.

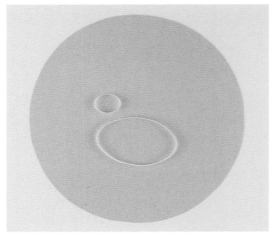

11 Place the head and body of the duckling on the center of the embossed paper.

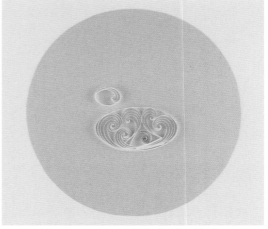

12 Add wave crescents inside the head and body to serve as feathers.

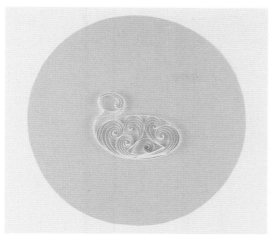

13 Make the neck of the duckling with the three curved lines.

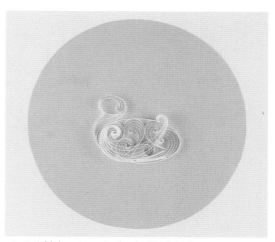

14 Add the wing onto the duckling's body.

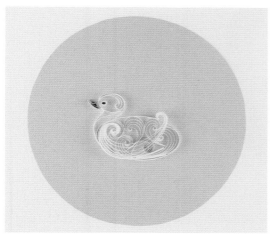

15 Add the eye and the beak onto the head of the duckling.

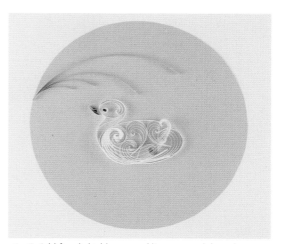

16 Add four light-blue curved lines as peach branches on the upper left of the picture.

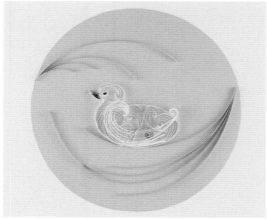

17 Add five peach branches on the bottom of the picture.

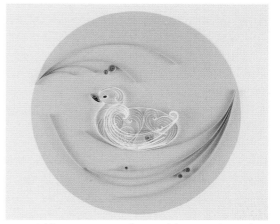

18 Add some grass-green loose coils between the peach branches as peach leaves. Complete the work by adjusting and fixing its contents with white latex.

2. Rain Water

Rain Water (*yushui*) as a solar term often falls on Feb. 18 to 20 each year. By then, the ice and snow will thaw with the warm east wind and there will be more rainfall, hence the name of Rain Water. During this period, the temperature goes up again, injecting life into everything on earth and heralding the advent of spring.

This work, with blue as its main tone, seeks to embody the color of water in an abstract way, with the colorful teardrop coils and raindrop loops showing the shapes of rain. In the picture stand several trees bathing in a spring drizzle. Vigorous and vibrant, they make the viewer feel as if spring were on its way here.

What is worth noticing is that paper slips of varied sizes are used in this work. The crescent tree branches are made of paper slips 1.5, 3 and 5 millimeters wide respectively, while the trunks are made of paper slips 5 millimeters wide and cut diagonally. This unique method of production shows the degree of freedom of Chinese-style paper quilling. While making your own works, you can also try to create different artistic effects through changing the size of paper slips.

Trunks: ⬤ crescent: basic crescent (the ends of the paper slip are thicker on one end and thinner on the other)

Branches: ⬤ crescent: basic crescent (three specifications)

Raindrops: ⬤⬤⬤◯◯◯◯◯ loop: raindrop loop; coil: teardrop coil

Background: white watercolor paper (suggested size: 27 by 27 centimeters)

1 Cut the 5-millimeter ultramarine-blue paper slip into two along the diagonal, one end thicker and the other thinner. Make 10 basic crescent trunks of different shapes and layers, each of them thick on one end and thin on the other.

2 Make a large number of basic crescent branches of different sizes, shapes and layers with paper slips 1.5, 3 and 5 millimeters wide.

3 Make many raindrop loops and teardrop coils as rainwater with violet, pink purple, pink green, light green, grass green, light blue and medium yellow paper slips.

4 Place three basic crescent elements from left to right, big to small, in the center, which serve as the trunk of the first tree.

5 Add several basic crescent elements to the bottom right of the trunk. They bend in an opposite direction to the first trunk. The elements can superimpose to form the trunk of the second tree.

6 Add several basic crescents as the trunk of the third tree to the left of the first trunk according to the picture.

7 Add smaller crescents above the three trunks as branches. Be careful that the branches face different directions and differ in distribution.

8 Add more branches and arrange them in picturesque disorder.

9 Add more crescents to make the branches look more three-dimensional. The branches on the right can be denser than those on the left so that they look in natural disorder.

10 Add raindrop loops and teardrop coils onto the bottom board as rainwater.

11 Add rainwater between the branches and right under the trees. Complete the work by adjusting the contents in the picture and fixing with white latex.

3. Waking of Insects

Waking of Insects (*jingzhe*) normally falls on Mar. 5 to 7 each year, meaning the awakening of insects from hibernation. By then, it has turned warmer. The rumbling of spring thunder wakes the insects from sleep. Peach flowers are in full blossom, orioles begin to sing, and everything on earth starts awakening.

In this work, the author reproduces the birth of spring plants with grass-green paper slips and presents this solar term with an ant just moving out of the dirt. The whole work is concise with smooth lines, giving the viewers a sense of freshness. The vivid-looking ant reaches forward with its two feelers, as if looking for the breath of spring. Just awakened by spring thunder, it moves out of the dirt with caution.

Materials and Elements

Plant roots: ● ○ crescent: wave crescent

Plant stems and leaves: ● lines: curved lines; scroll: long-tail scroll, basic scroll

Ant: ● coil: loose coil, tight coil, marquise coil; line: broken line

Background: white watercolor paper (suggested size: 27 by 27 centimeters)

1 Paste five grass-green paper slips together at the beginning end, the middle one (i.e. the third one) being the longest, the second and fourth shorter and the first and fifth the shortest. Scrape the paper slips on the most outside with small bamboo knife forcibly so that they curve.

2 Roll the paper slip along the curve with the slotted tool.

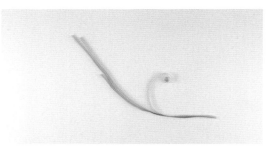

3 After the slotted tool is removed, the tail end of the slip forms a spiral.

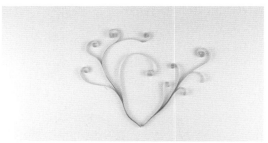

4 Treat four other paper slips similarly. The spirals, which are paired freely, can face either inward or outward. Then follow the previous steps and make a similar one with grass-green paper slips. They serve as the stems of the plant.

5 Make curved lines and scrolls (long-tail scrolls and basic scrolls) of different shapes in large quantities with grass-green paper slips. They will serve as the leaves on the stems.

6 Make five wave crescents of varied shapes, sizes and layers with grass-green and white paper slips, which will serve as the root of the plant.

7 Make a tight coil with the deep-red paper slip to serve as the head of the ant, a marquise coil as the thorax, and a loose coil as the abdomen. Make four broken lines to serve as the ant's feelers and feet.

8 Put different parts of the ant together and glue them with white latex.

9   Add wave crescents at the bottom of the picture to form the root of the plant.

10   Add a stem onto the root.

11   Add one more stem.

12   Add spiral-shaped leaves onto the stems.

13   Add more leaves here and there in the picture.

14   Place the ant at the bottom of the plant. Complete the work by adjusting and fixing its contents with white latex.

4. Vernal Equinox

Vernal Equinox (*chunfen*) is a solar term that means half of the spring has gone. It normally falls on Mar. 20 to 21 each year. On this day, the sun almost shines directly on the equator and the day is almost as long as the night across the world. After that day, the day becomes increasingly longer in the Northern Hemisphere and shorter in the Southern Hemisphere. In ancient times, Chinese emperors would offer sacrifices to the sun on that day and the people would start to sweep their ancestors' tombs. In addition, there are some other customs associated with this solar term, such as balancing eggs and flying kites.

Adopting the freehand genre from Chinese traditional painting, this work portrays a beautiful scene of mountains and rivers in spring. It consists of blue mountains in the distance and the green grassland nearby, the latter being separated into two by the purposefully-left blank space that symbolizes a river as well as "half" connoted by the Vernal Equinox. Overall, the colors used in this work display the charm of spring.

Materials and Elements

Waterfall: ● crescent: basic crescent

Mountains: ●●●●● crescent: irregular crescent

Grassland: ●●●●●●●● coil: teardrop coil, loose coil, tight coil

Background: white watercolor paper (suggested size: 27 by 27 centimeters), light-purple embossed paper (suggested size: 21 by 21 centimeters)

1 Make some teardrop coils of different sizes with paper slips in various shades of green.

2 Make a number of loose and tight coils of different sizes with paper slips in various shades of green and blue, mainly in the green colors.

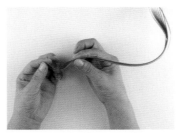

3 Make a 10-layered basic crescent with lake-blue paper slips, which will serve as the waterfall.

4 Paste 10 lake-blue paper slips at the beginning end and treat them in the same way the basic crescent is made.

5 Do not fix the tail end of the basic crescent with white latex. Instead, fix it by folding it as shown in the picture.

6 Fold it several times until four to five creases appear. Fix the tail end to form the shape of a mountain rock.

7 Make four rock shapes altogether. Put them together and fix them with white latex to form a complete mountain.

8 Make five more rock shapes of different postures with paper slips in shades of blue.

9 Stick the light-purple embossed paper onto the center of the white watercolor paper.

10 Add the waterfall onto the top of the picture.

11 Add the mountain to the right of the waterfall.

12 Add two rock shapes on the left of the waterfall.

13 Add rock shapes on the waterfall to create an impression of peaks rising upon each other.

14 Produce the outline of a river in the lower part of the picture with the tight and loose coils.

15 Keep adding tight and loose coils on both sides of the river to make the outline of the river more prominent.

16 Add tight and loose coils of various colors on the right side of the river.

17 Add more tight and loose coils on the left side of the river to form the whole stretch of the grassland.

18 Add smaller paper coils onto the grassland to make it look more luxuriant.

19 Add teardrop coils to the grassland to enrich its variations.

20 Stand some paper coils sideways and add them onto the grassland to increase the three-dimensional effect. Complete the work by adjusting its contents and fixing with white latex.

5. Pure Brightness

Pure Brightness (*qingming*) normally falls on Apr. 4 to 6 each year, meaning the weather turns clear and bright and all the things on earth begin to grow, because by this time it has become increasingly warmer, trees and grass have begun to sprout, and farmers have started spring ploughing. The customs associated with this solar term include going for a spring outing, having cold food and sweeping ancestors' tombs. Originally, Pure Brightness was only the name for this solar term, but gradually it has become a festival to cherish the memory of one's ancestors. Together with the Dragon Boat Festival, the Spring Festival and the Mid-Autumn Festival, it constitutes one of China's four traditional festivals.

Adopting the green and white colors of a Chinese cabbage, this work embodies the characteristics of spring ploughing. The cabbage is vivid-looking, consisting of only wave and teardrop crescents. The grasshopper on it symbolizes motion and the recovery of all things on earth. They contrast finely with each other.

Materials and Elements

Cabbage stems: ● loop: raindrop loop

Cabbage leaves: ● crescent: wave crescent

Cabbage root: ● line: curved line

Grasshopper: ● coil: tight coil; loop: raindrop loop; line: curved line, broken line

Background: white watercolor paper (suggested size: 27 by 27 centimeters)

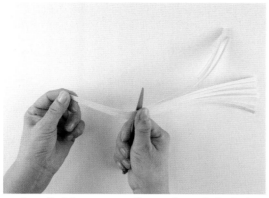

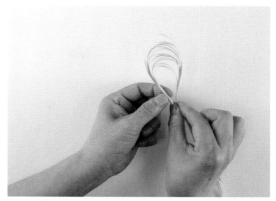

1 Paste 15 pink-green paper slips together at the beginning end with white latex. Scrape the end forcibly with a bamboo knife for several times until it bends naturally.

2 Hold the beginning end with one hand, and use another hand to draw the paper slips out with different lengths, thus leaving some space between the paper slips. Cut the redundant slips and fix them at the tail end with latex, forming a big raindrop loop.

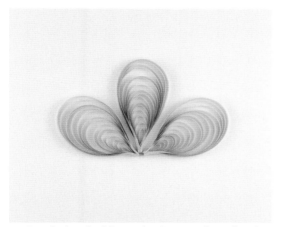

3 Paste both ends of the raindrop loop together. Follow this method and make three pink-green raindrop loops, which will serve as the stems of the cabbage.

4 Make more than 10 wave crescents of different sizes with the grass-green paper slips, each consisting of five layers. These will serve as the cabbage leaves.

5 Make a continuous curved element in the form of "8" with the light-green paper slips. The curved lines are arranged from big to small, with some of them remaining loose at the end. This will serve as the cabbage's root.

6 Make the body parts of the grasshopper with the deep-red paper slips. Make a tight coil as its head and thigh, a raindrop loop as its body, curved lines as its feelers, and broken lines as its calf and feet.

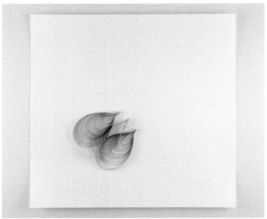

7 Pile up the cabbage stems on the lower-left corner of the background paper. Place one raindrop loop in between the two raindrop loops.

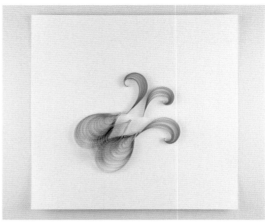

8 Place three grass-green wave crescents on the upper right of the cabbage stems to serve as cabbage leaves.

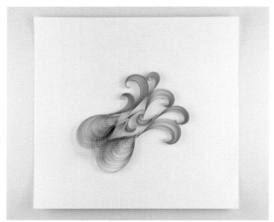

9 Add more grass-green wave crescents around the cabbage leaves.

10 Pile up the second layer of grass-green wave crescents above the cabbage leaves to make the leaves look more three-dimensional and fuller.

11 Add root to the cabbage.

12 Join the body parts of the grasshopper together and place it on the cabbage stem. Complete the work by adjusting and fixing its contents with white latex.

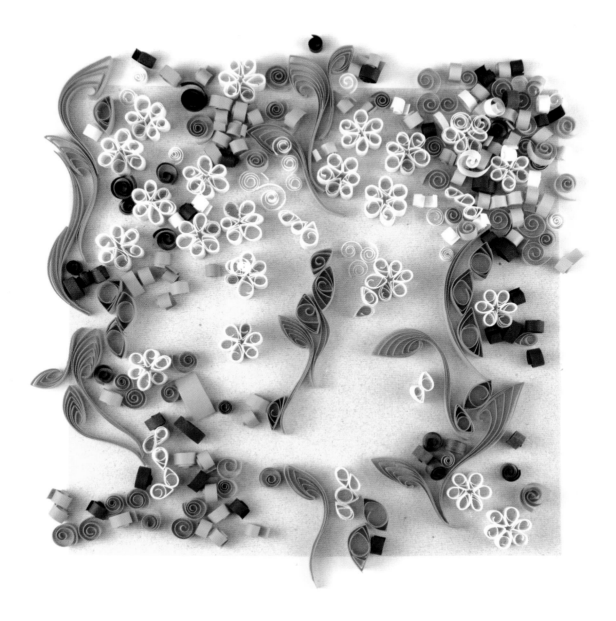

6. Grain Rain

Grain Rain (*guyu*) normally falls on Apr. 19 to 21. It is the last solar term in spring, meaning the rain gives birth to all grains. By then, the cold weather is almost over and the temperature rises rapidly with a lot of rainfall, which benefits the growth of grains and other crops. In China, this is a fine time for tealeaf picking, as the tealeaves are plump and tender, freshly green, fragrant and nutritious.

This work consists mainly of green leaves and teardrops. The supplementary white flowers show a drizzling spring scene during this period. Many green loose coils are piled up, resembling both raindrops and paddy kernels. The whole work is elegant, fresh and vigorous.

Materials and Elements

Raindrops: ⬤⬤⬤⬤⬤○ coil: loose coil

Smaller leaves: ⬤ coil: half-circle coil, marquise coil

Bigger leaves: ⬤ crescent: *ruyi* scepter-shaped crescent

Plant stems: ⬤ crescent: S crescent, basic crescent

Flower petals: ○⬤ coil: teardrop coil

Background: white watercolor paper (suggested size: 27 by 27 centimeters), yellow-gray embossed paper (suggested size: 21 by 21 centimeters)

1 Make a wave crescent with the grass-green paper slips.

2 Scrape the tail of the wave crescent with a small bamboo knife until it bends toward the opposite of the crescent.

3 Hold the tail end of the crescent with one hand, and pinch another end with the other hand to make it an acute angle.

4 The *ruyi* scepter-shaped crescent is completed.

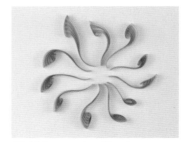

5 Make more than 10 *ruyi* scepter-shaped crescents of different layers and sizes to serve as bigger leaves.

6 Paste three grass-green paper slips at the beginning end. Scrape the end with a small bamboo knife to make it bend.

7 About 3 centimeters away from the beginning end, scrape the slip with a small bamboo knife in the opposite direction to make the paper slip bend in the shape of an S.

8 Pull the paper slips downward into different lengths.

9 Cut the redundant slips and paste the tail end with white latex. The S crescent is completed.

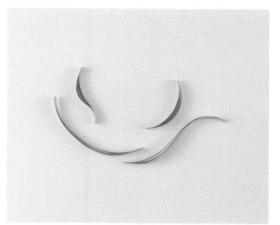

10 Make two basic crescents and two S crescents with the grass-green paper slips. Each crescent consists of three to four paper slips. They will serve as the stems of the plants.

11 Make more than 10 half-circle coils and marquise coils with the grass-green paper slips by pinching; these will serve as smaller leaves.

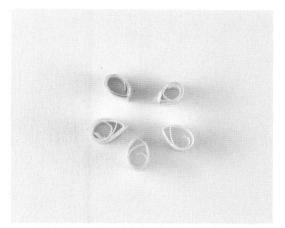

12 Make four to five white teardrop coils and one pink teardrop coil with the white and pink paper slips; these will serve as flower petals.

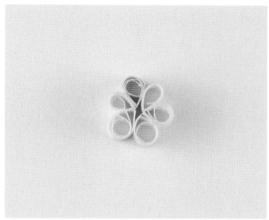

13 Put the petals together to form a flower.

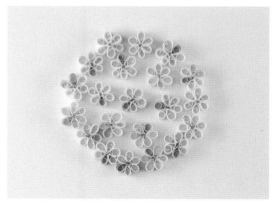

14 Make more than 20 flowers with the white and pink paper slips. More teardrop coils can be made as petals for later use.

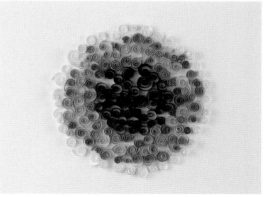

15 Make a lot of loose coils with paper slips in various shades of green and white paper slips to serve as raindrops. The white loose coils used in this work are made with two specifications of paper slips: 5 millimeters and 3 millimeters.

16 Paste the yellow-gray embossed paper onto the center of the background paper.

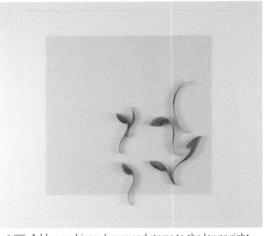

17 Add some bigger leaves and stems to the lower-right corner of the picture.

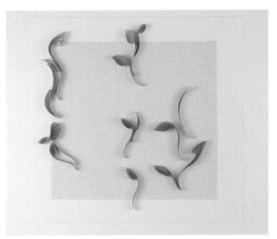

18 Keep adding bigger leaves and stems to the upper left of the picture.

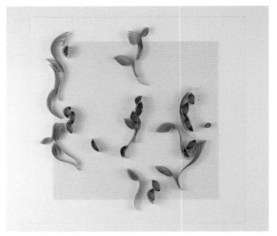

19 Add smaller leaves among bigger leaves.

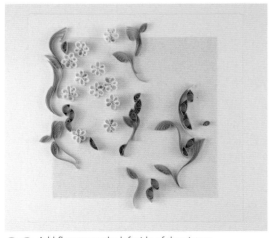

20 Add flowers on the left side of the picture.

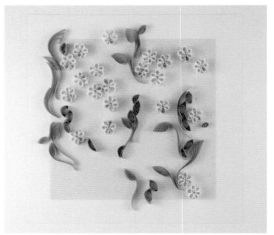

21 Add flowers on the right side of the picture.

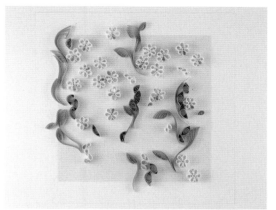

22 Add some more petals, which can be placed on the flowers to make the picture look more three-dimensional.

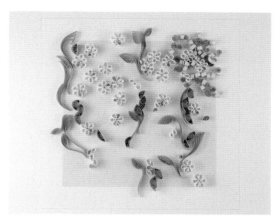

23 Place some pink-green loose coils on the upper-right corner of the picture. The coils can be arranged head-on or sideways or upon each other. Adjust them so they look naturally piled up.

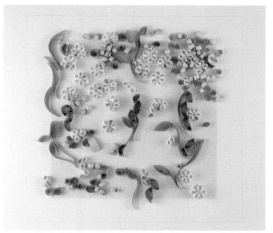

24 Arrange some light-green and grass-green loose coils on the upper-left and lower-left corners of the picture.

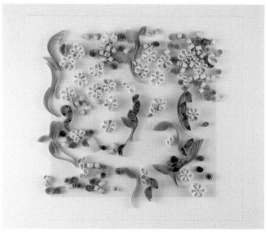

25 Add some olive-green and grass-green loose coils onto the picture.

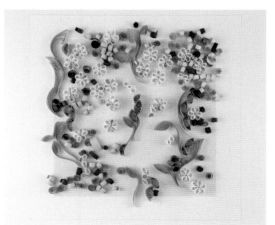

26 Keep adding some dark-green loose coils here and there in the picture.

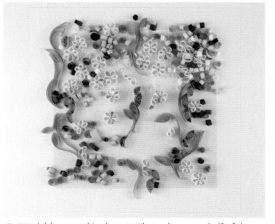

27 Add some white loose coils on the upper half of the picture. Complete the work by adjusting its contents and fixing with white latex.

7. Beginning of Summer

Beginning of Summer (*lixia*) normally falls on May 5 to 7 each year. It is the first solar term in summer, symbolizing the end of the spring and the official start of the hot summer. By then, there are more thunderstorms and crops have been growing rapidly. On this day in ancient times, Chinese emperors, accompanied by their officials and officers, would host a ceremony to greet the advent of summer. The ordinary people, on the other hand, will hang eggs, eat eggs and weigh themselves.

In this work, a school of little fishes vie with each other in surfacing the water to breathe the fresh air due to the reduced air pressure caused by the thunderstorm. There are all together 12 fishes in the picture, symbolizing the transmigration of the 12 months in a year. The whole work is concise in composition and bright in color, active and lovely.

Materials and Elements

Fish bodies: ⚪🔘⚫⚫ loop: basic loop; line: curved line

Fish scales: 🔘⚫⚫⚫ line: zigzag line

Fish eyes: ⚪⚫🔘⚪ coil: tight coil

Background: white watercolor paper (suggested size: 27 by 27 centimeters), orange-yellow embossed paper (suggested size: 21 by 21 centimeters)

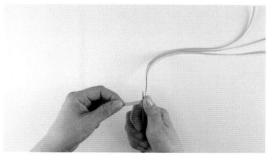

1 Paste three grass-green paper slips at the beginning end with white latex. Scrape them with a small bamboo knife to make them bend.

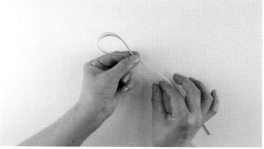

2 Hold the beginning end and the point at about 10 centimeters from the beginning end with one hand and pull out three paper slips of different lengths with another hand, thus leaving some space between the three slips.

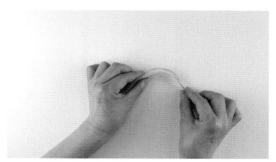

3 Cut the redundant part, leaving only about 1 centimeter as the fish tail. Fix it with white latex. Then hold the fish tail with one hand and pinch to form a sharp fish head with the other hand.

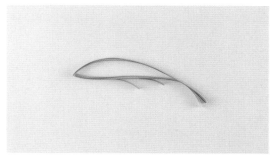

4 Add two curved lines of 1 centimeter in length onto the belly of the fish as the fins. This completes the body of the fish.

5 Make a tight coil with the black and light-yellow paper slips to serve as the fish eye.

6 Make a section of zigzag line with the lemon-yellow paper slip to serve as the fish scale.

7 Place the eyes and scales into the fish bodies. Then make a total of 12 small fishes with paper slips of different colors.

8 Paste the orange-yellow embossed paper onto the center of the white watercolor paper.

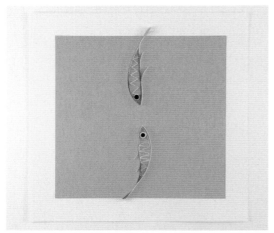

9 Add two grass-green fishes in the 12 o'clock and 6 o'clock directions.

10 Add two white fishes in the 3 o'clock and 9 o'clock directions.

11 Add four fishes on the left side of the picture, with their colors crisscrossing each other.

12 Add the remaining fishes on the right side of the picture, with their colors crisscrossing each other. Complete the work by adjusting its contents and fixing with white latex.

8. Grain Budding

Grain Budding (*xiaoman*) normally falls on May 20 to 22 each year. By then, the crops in northern China, like wheat, have started to grow fuller, but not yet ripened. Legend has it that this day is the birthday of the God of Silkworms. Therefore, in southern China, such as Jiangsu and Zhejiang provinces, people have made that day a festival to worship the Silkworm God. As the earliest country to plant mulberry trees and raise silkworms, China has long focused on the silk weaving industry. For this reason, in old times, both the ruling class and the ordinary people showed great respect to the God of Silkworms.

This period is perfect for growing rice, as the abundant rainfall has filled the farming land with water. This work depicts the scene of fishes swimming in an overflowing river. The whole work is round in composition, connoting complete happiness.

Materials and Elements

1 Make a small five-layer raindrop loop with the light-blue paper slips. Then wrap it with another light-blue paper slip, leaving some length on both ends of the slip. Be careful to leave some space between the loop and the outermost paper slip that wraps it.

2 Stick the outermost paper slip and the raindrop loop together with white latex. The two small sections of paper slips on both ends will serve as the tail of the fish.

3 Cut two sections of the light-blue paper slip of about 1 centimeter in length, and paste them onto each side of the fish as fins.

4 Make seven fishes using the same method.

5 Make seven tight coils with the deep-red and white paper slips as the fish eyes.

6 Make some basic crescents and S crescents of different lengths, shapes and layers with the white paper slips.

7 Make more wave crescents of different shapes with the white paper slips.

8 Paste the round deep-green embossed paper onto the center of the white background paper.

9 Add two wave crescents in the center of the picture.

10 Add two more wave crescents on the upper part of the picture.

11 Add several longer crescents and S crescents among the wave crescents.

12 Keep adding crescents until they fill the whole picture.

13 Add two small fishes with their heads facing each other in the center of the picture.

14 Add three small fishes at the bottom of the picture, with their heads facing left.

15 Add two small fishes on the top of the picture, with their heads facing right.

16 Add eyes to the fishes. Complete the work by adjusting its contents and fixing with white latex.

9. Grain in Ear

Grain in Ear (*mangzhong*) normally falls on Jun. 5 to 7 each year. It literally means harvesting crops with awns on them and sowing seeds for autumn crops. Therefore, it is the busiest time of the year for farmers. During this period, such activities as bidding farewell to the Goddess of Flowers and making plum drinks are popular.

This work depicts this solar term with wheat to be harvested. The golden ears of wheat containing perfect kernels look vivid and real. The many ears form a stretch of wheat land, reminding people of waves of wheat in the wind. The whole work, well-spaced and complete in composition, expresses the author's respect of farmers for their hard work and the wish for a bumper harvest.

Materials and Elements

Wheat kernels: coil: marquise coil

Wheat ears: line: broken line, curved line; coil: marquise coil

Wheat awns: line: curved line

Background: white watercolor paper (suggested size: 27 by 27 centimeters)

1 Make 12 smaller loose coils with the medium-yellow paper slips.

2 Pinch the loose coils into a spindle shape with both hands to form a marquise coil, which will serve as the wheat kernels.

3 Treat the 12 loose coils in step 1 in the same way.

4 Take out two light-brown paper slips of different lengths. Fold the longer one in half and wrap the shorter one with it.

5 Fold a small section of the longer paper slip on the right along the shorter paper slip. Paste this section with white latex.

6 Add a kernel onto the small section and wrap the kernel with the longer paper slip on the right. Fix the kernel with white latex.

7 Add six kernels following steps 5 and 6 to complete the right half of the wheat ear. Follow the same method to make the left side of the ear.

8 Cut twelve sections of curved lines, each about 2 centimeters long, out of the light-brown paper slips; these will serve as the awns of wheat.

9 Paste the 12 awns onto the 12 wheat kernels.

10 The wheat ear is finished.

11 Follow the same method to make 10 wheat ears of different sizes.

12 Continue to make more than 20 wheat ears of different sizes with light yellow and medium yellow as the supplementary colors.

13 Wrap a kernel made of the light-yellow paper slip with the medium-yellow paper slip to form a single group of kernel and awn.

14 Make more than 20 independent wheat kernels and awns following the same method.

15 Add two light-brown wheat ears in the center of the picture. Add four light-brown wheat ears to the lower-right corner of the picture to form a group.

16 Add two groups of light-brown ears to the lower-left corner of the picture, two in one group.

17 Add some medium-yellow ears in the center of the picture.

18 Keep adding medium-yellow ears on the right side of the picture.

19 Add more medium-yellow ears on the right and left sides of the picture.

20 Add some smaller medium-yellow ears into the gaps in the picture.

21 Add some independent wheat kernels and awns above the wheat ears on top of the picture.

22 Add some independent wheat ears and awns in the center of the picture, in imitation of wheat kernels scattered on the ground. Complete the work by adjusting its contents and fixing with white latex.

10. Summer Solstice

Like Winter Solstice, Summer Solstice (*xiazhi*), which normally falls on Jun. 21 to 22 each year, is a solar term reflecting seasonal changes. It is the earliest of the 24 solar terms that has been designated as such. As far back as the seventh century BC, Chinese ancestors have established Summer Solstice by way of measuring sun shadows with an ancient time-recording instrument. On this day, the sun's rays are directly overhead along the Tropic of Cancer and the daytime in the Northern Hemisphere is the longest of the year. This period coincides with wheat harvesting and popular customs include celebrating a good harvest and offering sacrifices to one's ancestors.

This work shows the characteristics of this solar term with a scene at dusk. The trees are luxuriant and vigorous. The sun still hangs in the sky casting colorful afterglow down on the earth, even though it is toward evening.

Materials and Elements

Bigger leaves: ●●● loop: raindrop loop; coil: teardrop coil; crescent: basic crescent, wave crescent

Smaller leaves: ●●● coil: teardrop coil

Tree branches: ●●●● line: curved line; crescent: S crescent

Sunlight: ●●●●●●●●● coil: tight coil

Background: white watercolor paper (suggested size: 27 by 27 centimeters), magenta embossed paper (suggested size: 21 by 21 centimeters)

1 Make tight coils of different sizes with papers slips in various shades of blue and green. Wrap each coil with paper slips in various shades of yellow in imitation of sunlight.

2 Make more than 10 teardrop coils of different sizes with the paper slips in various shades of blue, which will serve as the smaller leaves.

3 Make two S crescents and some curved lines with paper slips in various shades of blue, which will serve as the tree branches.

4 Make two teardrop coils with paper slips in various shades of blue, which will serve as the bigger leaves.

5 Make three teardrop coils with paper slips in shades of blue. Here the remaining paper slips can still be used to make basic crescents and wave crescents inside the teardrop coils. In the picture are three other bigger leaves. You can also give full play to your own creativity in producing elements you like.

6 Make some basic crescents and teardrop coils with paper slips in various shades of blue to serve as fillers inside the bigger leaves.

7 After the five bigger leaves and filler are all done, the next step is to put the fillers into the bigger leaves.

8 Put the fillers inside the bigger leaves. The technique the author uses here is not normally found in other places of this book. By superimposing the elements and using smaller elements to fill in the bigger elements, the author shows the flexibility in the production of Chinese paper quilling works.

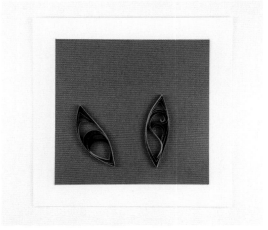

9 Stick the magenta embossed paper onto the center of the white background paper.

10 Add two bigger leaves on the bottom of the picture.

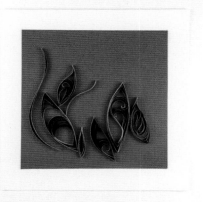

11 Keep adding the remaining three bigger leaves. You can also add a teardrop coil on the right side of the bigger tree on the lower left of the picture to enrich the whole picture.

12 Add a longer S crescent to the leftmost side of the picture and a shorter S crescent on the right side of the bigger leaf on the left.

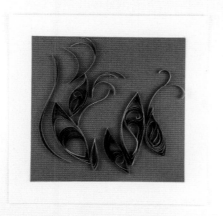

13 Arrange three groups of curved lines above the bigger leaves.

14 Add darker-blue teardrop coils at the bottom of the picture.

15 Keep adding lighter-blue teardrop coils.

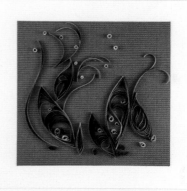

16 Add some tight coils on the upper-left corner of the picture in imitation of the afterglow.

17 Add some tight coils on the upper-right corner of the picture.

18 Keep adding tight coils of assorted colors here and there in the picture and arrange them in a picturesque disorder. Complete the work by adjusting its contents and fixing with white latex.

11. Slight Heat

Slight Heat (*xiaoshu*) normally falls on Jul. 6 to 8 each year, meaning the weather is becoming hotter, but still not the hottest. By then, the temperature has risen, the trees make pleasant shade, and the crops grow robustly as the midsummer starts. In southern China, the rainy season is over and the summer drought begins. In northern China, however, the rainy season has started and people are busy preventing waterlogging.

In ancient China, Slight Heat was divided into three periods and the second period was known as "crickets living in the house," which means that the cricket hides itself in the corner of the yard to get away from the heat. This work depicts such a special scene: Two crickets lie on a big pumpkin to avoid the summer heat. The orange pumpkin resembles the scorching sun in color and shape.

Materials and Elements

Pumpkin sections: ⚪⚫⚫ loop: irregular raindrop loop

Pumpkin stem: ⚫⚫ crescent: irregular crescent

Crickets: ⚫⚫⚫⚫ coil: tight coil, loose coil, triangular coil, marquise coil, irregular coil; line: curved line

Background: white watercolor paper (suggested size: 27 by 27 centimeters)

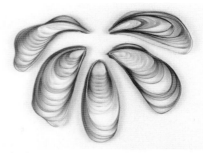

1 Make five big raindrop loops with the lemon-yellow, deep-red and orange-red paper slips. Each of them consists of more than 10 layers.

2 Make the five raindrop loops irregular in shape as is shown in the picture by pinching and pasting; these will serve as the different sections of the pumpkin.

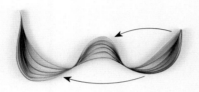

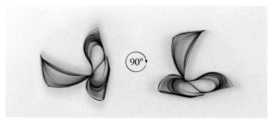

3 Arrange an olive-green paper slip in the middle of the five light-brown paper slips. Make three continuous basic crescents as is shown in the picture. Paste both ends of the continuous crescents, as well as the conjunctions where the crescents meet.

4 Make the three continuous crescents into the shape of a stem using the techniques of bending, pinching, and pasting by referring to the arrows shown in step 3. The two conjunctions are pasted together.

5 Make different body parts of the cricket with the black and burnt umber paper slips. Use tight coil and curved line for the feeler, loose coil for the head, triangular coil for the thorax, marquise coil for the wing, and comma-shaped irregular coil for the six feet.

6 Piece together the parts of the first cricket and get it fixed. Use the same method to make the second cricket with the black, olive-green and dark-green paper slips.

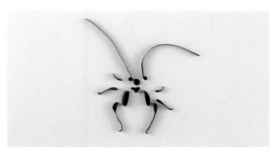

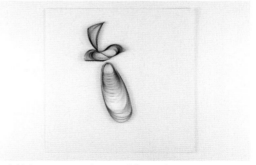

7 Place the middle section of the pumpkin in the center of the picture.

8 Add the stem onto the top of this section.

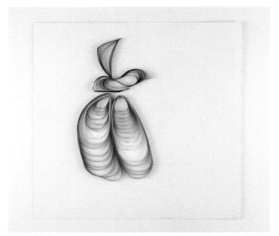

9 Add the second section of the pumpkin to the left of the first section.

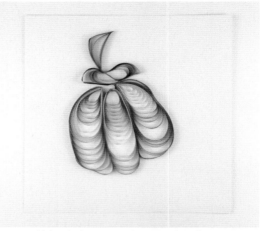

10 Add the third section to the right of the first section.

11 Add another section to the far left.

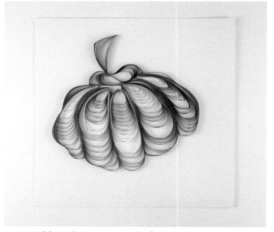

12 Add another section to the far right, completing the pumpkin.

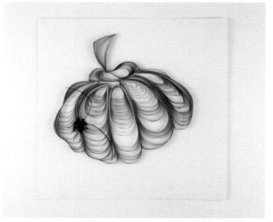

13 Place a cricket on the left half of the pumpkin.

14 Place the other cricket on the right half of the pumpkin. Complete the work by adjusting its contents and fixing with white latex.

12. Great Heat

Great Heat (*dashu*) refers to the hottest days in a year. This solar term normally falls on Jul. 22 to 24 each year. By then, the temperature is the highest and the crops grow the fastest. However, it is also a period most frequently visited by natural disasters. The popular customs include drinking medical herb tea, drying gingers and burning incense to pray for a good harvest, etc.

This work uses the cicada, one of the most common insects in summer, to represent this solar term. Cicadas singing in forests is a major symbol of a hot summer. Using simple elements, the author creates a vivid-looking cicada, reminding viewers of the boisterous chirping in great summer heat.

Materials and Elements

Cicada body: ●● crescent: basic crescent

Cicada head: ● ◯ loop: oval loop

Cicada eyes: ● ◯ crescent: basic crescent

Designs on cicada's head: ● ◯ crescent: spiral crescent; line: curved line

Cicada's wings: ◯ loop: irregular loop, raindrop loop

Tree leaves: ◯◯ crescent: wave crescent

Background: white watercolor paper (suggested size: 27 by 27 centimeters)

1 Arrange four scarlet paper slips inside five dark-red paper
slips. Make a nine-layer crescent with them.

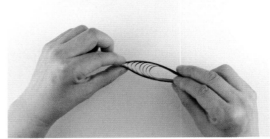

2 Hold the open end of the crescent with one hand, and
pinch the arc on the other end with fingers to form a sharp
angle, which will serve as the body of the cicada.

3 Arrange four dark-red paper slips inside one light-yellow
paper slip. Make a five-layer oval loop with them as the
head of the cicada.

4 Arrange four dark-red paper slips inside one light-yellow
paper slip. Make two smaller crescents with them to serve
as the eyes of the cicada.

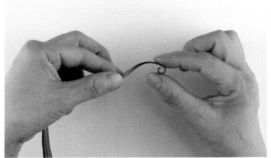

5 Superimpose five scarlet paper slips, paste their beginning
ends together with white latex, and then roll the end up.

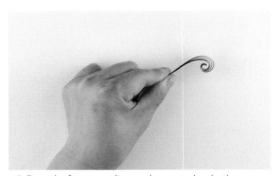

6 Draw the five paper slips one by one and make them curve
proportionately, leaving some space between them.

7 Leave about 2 centimeters and cut the redundant part.
Paste the tail end with white latex and roll it in the
opposite direction of the beginning end.

8 This is the finished spiral crescent.

9 Follow steps 5 through 8 and make another similar spiral crescent. Add the curved lines made with the light-yellow paper slips as shown in the picture. These are the designs on the cicada's head.

10 Superimpose four light-yellow paper slips. Paste their beginning ends together with white latex. Pinch it at about 10 centimeters from the beginning end.

11 Pinch the shape three centimeters from the beginning end.

12 Cut the redundant part as is shown in the picture to form an irregular loop. This will serve as the outline of the cicada wing.

13 Make some raindrop loops with the light-yellow paper slips.

14 Place the raindrop loops inside the cicada wing.

15 Follow steps 10 to 14 and make another similar cicada wing with the light-yellow paper slips.

16 Make more than 10 four-layer wave crescents with the light-green paper slips.

17 Make more than 10 four-layer wave crescents with the light-blue paper slips.

18 Put together the cicada's head and body as is shown in the picture.

19 Fill the outline of the cicada's head with the spiral crescents.

20 Add two eyes on the cicada's head.

21 Add a pair of wings to the cicada's body.

22 Add several light-blue wave crescents around the cicada to serve as leaves. Be careful that these crescents face different directions.

23 Keep adding light-blue wave crescents.

24 Between the light-blue leaves add some light-green leaves. The leaves can superimpose on each other. Complete the work by adjusting its contents and fixing with white latex.

13. Beginning of Autumn

Beginning of Autumn (*liqiu*) normally falls on Aug. 7 to 9 each year. By then, the west wind has blown away the summer heat. It is getting cooler every day and leaves start to fall from the Chinese parasol tree. In ancient time, the emperors, together with their officials and officers, would offer sacrifices to greet autumn and the people would celebrate this solar term as a festival. The Chinese people usually weigh themselves on this day and then compare the result with their weights on the Beginning of Summer. Autumn is considered an ideal time for them to make up for their weight losses in summer.

This work presents this solar term with the chrysanthemum, a flower unique of autumn. In traditional Chinese culture, the chrysanthemum is regarded as a hermit, as it blooms alone in autumn, instead of competing with other flowers in spring and summer. Using basic loops and their variations alone, this work displays a vivid-looking chrysanthemum in full blossom.

Chrysanthemum petals: loop: irregular loop

Chrysanthemum stems and leaves: ⚫🔘 loop: irregular loop

Background: white watercolor paper (suggested size: 27 by 27 centimeters)

1 Make some basic loops of assorted sizes and layers with the dark-green and grass-green paper slips. Use such techniques as rolling, scraping, pinching and pressing to produce different shapes. They will serve as the stems and leaves of the chrysanthemum.

2 Follow the methods in step 1 and make the petals of the chrysanthemum with the lemon-yellow paper slips.

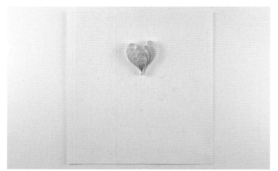

3 Arrange some smaller petals on the upper-middle area of the picture in the form of a heart. This will serve as the central part of the chrysanthemum.

4 Add longer petals on both sides of the heart.

5 Keep adding petals that grow downward. Be careful to make the petals roll in different directions to create a more natural effect.

6 Then fill the blank space with petals to make the flower look fuller, completing the chrysanthemum.

7 Add green stems and leaves right beneath the chrysanthemum as is shown in the picture.

8 Add stems and leaves on the right side of the picture.

9 Continue to add stems and leaves on the left side of the picture.

10 Add some outreaching stems and leaves in appropriate places in the picture so that the whole work looks complete and fuller.

11 Add two groups of petals between the stems and leaves as decoration.

12 Complete the work by adjusting its contents and fixing with white latex.

14. Limit of Heat

Meaning the termination of summer heat, Limit of Heat (*chushu*) normally falls on Aug. 22 to 24 each year. It is a solar term that reflects temperature changes and marks the end of summer. By then, the weather turns cooler every day and people begin to appreciate the beauty of autumn in outings and travels.

This work depicts this solar term with the lotus flower, a bloom one cannot fail to appreciate in midsummer. The budding flowers on the left and the blooming flowers on the right show that everything starts to fall after it has reached zenith. It is a rule of nature that flowers, once in full bloom, will then start to wither. And this is exactly what happens after Limit of Heat.

Materials and Elements

Lotus flowers: ● loop: half-circle loop, raindrop loop, heart-shaped loop

Lotus leaves and stems: ● ● loop: raindrop loop; line: curved line

Waves: ○ crescent: basic crescent; line: curved line

Background: white watercolor paper (suggested size: 27 by 27 centimeters), sky-blue embossed paper (suggested size: 21 by 21 centimeters)

1 Make a raindrop loop with one grass-green and two dark-green paper slips.

2 Follow the same method and make more than 20 raindrop loops of different sizes to serve as the components of the lotus leaf.

3 Make a nine-layer raindrop loop with nine pink paper slips.

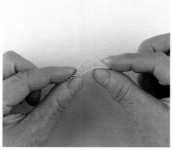

4 Pinch both ends of the pink raindrop loop with your fingers and make it into a shape like curved marquise coil.

5 Make more pink raindrop loops of varied sizes and pinch them into half circles or hearts. They will be used as the petals of the lotus flowers.

6 Make some curved lines and basic crescent as waves with the white paper slips.

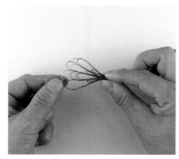

7 Wrap four green raindrop loops with a grass-green paper slip, which will serve as the lotus leave.

8 Treat other raindrop loops in the same way and put them together to form a complete lotus leaf.

9 Stick together a grass-green and a dark-green paper slip. Then enclose these lotus leaf components with the double-layered slip.

10 Paste the enclosure with white latex and adjust it to form a whole piece of lotus leaf. Arrange it on the lower-left corner of the sky-blue embossed paper.

11 Follow steps 7 to 10 to make another smaller lotus leaf and arrange it on the upper-right corner of the sky-blue embossed paper.

12 Bend the grass-green and dark-green paper slips and use them as the stem of the lotus flower. Arrange it onto the lower-left corner of the lotus leaf. Add a green raindrop loop to the lower-right corner of the picture.

13 Make a blooming lotus flower with the pink loops already completed. Arrange it on the lotus leaf on the upper-right corner.

14 Add a withering lotus flower onto the stem on the lower-left corner and a falling petal on the lotus leaf.

15 Arrange the white waves here and there in the picture and fix them with white latex to finish the piece.

15. White Dew

White Dew (*bailu*) is a solar term that reflects temperature changes in nature. It normally falls on Sept. 7 to 9 each year. By then, the autumn chill is gradually taking hold. The moisture in the night air condenses due to the morning cold, forming dense little dews on grass and leaves, which, reflecting the morning sunshine, look crystal clear. This is known as "White Dew."

The author uses the image of a white egret, which is homophonic to this solar term in Chinese, for embodiment. Together with some reeds that flower in September, this creates a vivid-looking picture of a white egret standing in the chill of autumn. The egret, consisting only of several elements, looks neat and concise.

Materials and Elements

Egret: ◯ crescent: wave crescent, basic crescent

Feathers of the egret: ◯ coil: loose coil

Eye of the egret: ● coil: tight coil

Reed stalks: ◉◉ loop: raindrop loop

Reed catkins and underbrush: ◉ line: curved line

Background: white watercolor paper (suggested size: 27 by 27 centimeters), grass-green embossed paper (suggested size: a piece of round paper with a diameter of 21 centimeters)

1 Make basic crescents and wave crescents with the white paper slips according to the picture to form the body of the egret. Leave a relatively long section of the paper slip on both ends of the basic crescent at the top and on one end of the basic crescent at the bottom.

2 Make curving reed catkins with the pink paper slips. Paste one end together while leaving the other end in its naturally irregular form.

3 Make a number of raindrop loops with the flesh color and orange-red paper slips, leaving a section of the slip on one end to serve as the reed stalk.

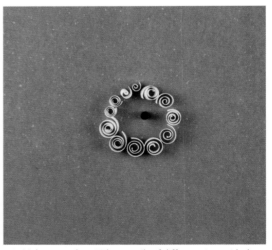

4 Make more than 10 loose coils of different sizes with the white paper slips, which serve as the egret's feathers. Make a tight coil with a black paper slip, which serves as the egret's eye.

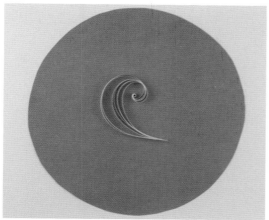

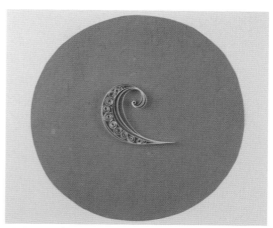

5 Paste the round grass-green embossed paper onto the center of the white background. Then arrange the body of the egret in its center.

6 Arrange the white loose coils inside the egret's body as the feathers, with the bigger ones in the middle and smaller ones on both sides.

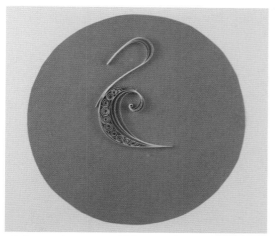

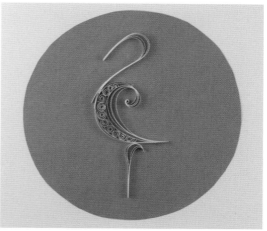

7 Arrange the crescent with longer ends onto the top of the egret's body as its head and neck.

8 Add the crescent with one longer end below the body to imitate the erect foot of the egret.

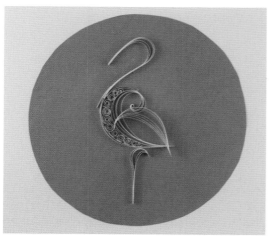

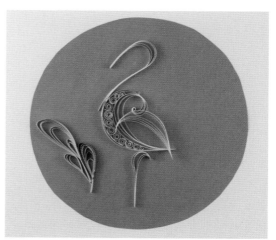

9 Add a crescent to the body to form the egret's wing.

10 Add three raindrop loops to the left side of the egret.

11 Add three raindrop loops to the right side of the egret.

12 Keep adding raindrop loops to the right side of the egret to form luxuriant reeds. The rings can be partially overlapping.

13 Add some pink curved lines at the foot of the egret as underbrush.

14 Add the remaining pink curved lines on top of the reeds on the right as reed catkins to enhance the autumn atmosphere. Complete the work by adjusting the contents and fixing with white latex.

16. Autumnal Equinox

Autumnal Equinox (*qiufen*) normally falls on Sept. 23 to 24 each year, meaning mid-autumn. On that day, the center of the sun spends a roughly equal amount of time above and below the horizon at every location on the earth, so night and day are about the same length. The customs related to this solar term include offering sacrifices to the moon, eating autumn vegetables for health, having dumplings and flying kites.

This work presents this solar term with blooming dandelions and their flowers dancing in the autumn air. The green stems and leaves of the dandelions are in the form of an arc, resembling the bright moon in the sky and metaphorically referring to the custom of offering sacrifices to the moon. The whole work is ingenious in composition, fresh in color and graceful in posture.

Materials and Elements

Dandelion petals: line: curved line

Dandelion receptacles: ◯ loop: basic loop

Dandelion stems and leaves: ● ● ● crescent: basic crescent

Background: white watercolor paper (suggested size: 27 by 27 centimeters)

1 Make 10 basic crescents of different lengths, layers and radians with paper slips in various shades of green.

2 Make slender loops with the white paper slips as the receptacles of the dandelions.

3 Cut the white and gray paper slips into sections. Fold the sections in half and paste the folding places with white latex. Scrape each of the paper slips until they form an arc and spread like a fan. They will serve as the petals of the dandelions. Make four big dandelion petals.

4 Follow the method in step 3 and make a large number of smaller dandelion petals with the white and gray paper slips.

5 Add green crescents to the top of the picture as the stem and leaves of the dandelions.

6 Continue to add crescents at the bottom of the picture, forming a cycle with the crescents on top.

7 Add crescents on the left side of the picture to form bigger arcs.

8 Add some dandelion stems and leaves to the lower-right corner of the picture.

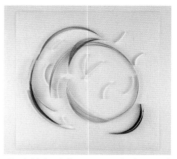

9 Add dandelion receptacles here and there in the picture.

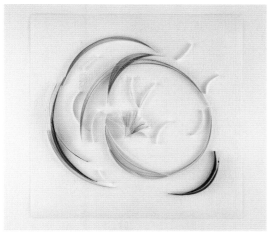

10 Add two bigger dandelion petals to the center of the picture, with one partially overlapping the other.

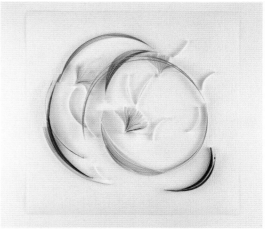

11 Add the remaining two bigger petals beneath the green stems and leaves to create a three-dimensional effect.

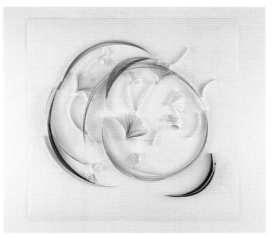

12 Add some smaller dandelion petals onto the receptacles.

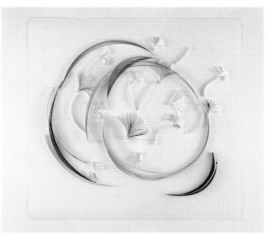

13 Continue to add dandelion petals here and there in the picture.

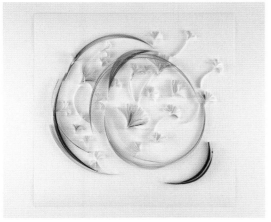

14 When adding petals of different sizes, try to make some petals overlap each other to create a hierarchical effect.

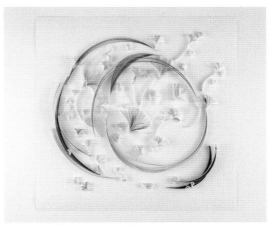

15 Add the smallest petals here and there in the picture. Complete the whole work by adjusting its contents and fixing with white latex.

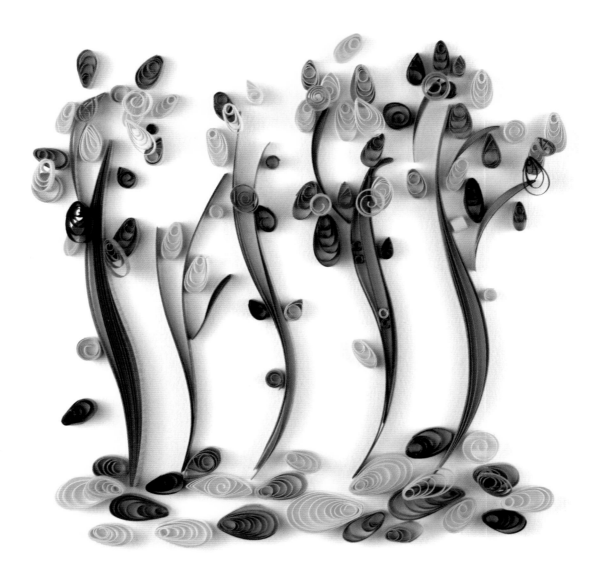

17. Cold Dew

Cold Dew (*hanlu*) normally falls on Oct. 8 to 9 each year. By then, it is already the depth of autumn. The temperature becomes even lower than that in White Dew and the dews on the ground are going to frost. Although White Dew, Cold Dew and Frost Descent are all indicative of moisture condensation, Cold Dew means the transition from being cool to cold. Plants on earth begin to die out and it is time to enter a severe winter.

This work presents this solar term with several trees shedding leaves. The leaves on the branches are no longer as dense as in summer and the falling leaves are gradually covering the ground. Dew hangs between leaves, ready to frost, which presents a desolate scene of late autumn.

Materials and Elements

Tree trunks and branches: ●●●●● crescent: basic crescent, S crescent

Leaves: ●●●●●●●● coil: teardrop coil

Dew: ●●●●●●●● coil: loose coil

Background: white watercolor paper (suggested size: 27 by 27 centimeters)

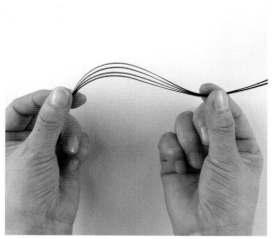

1 Make a long S crescent with the deep-gray paper slips.

2 This long S crescent will be used as tree trunk.

3 Make altogether five long and multi-layered S crescents with the deep-gray, earth-yellow, light-brown and burnt-umber paper slips. They will serve as the tree trunks. Make some shorter basic crescents and S crescents with fewer layers to serves as tree branches. Loop elements can also be used as tree branches.

4 Make some loose coils of varied sizes with paper slips of different colors. They will serve as dew.

5 Make a large number of teardrop coils with paper slips in various shades of yellow, brown and gray. They will serve as leaves.

6 Lay some teardrop coils at the bottom of the picture as falling leaves. Be careful that the colors match each other and the locations are well-arranged.

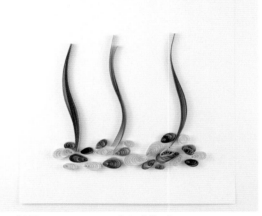

7 Continue to add teardrop coils to show the abundance of the falling leaves.

8 Add S crescents on top of the falling leaves to serve as three tree trunks.

9 Continue to add the other two trunks between the first ones.

10 Add branches to the trunks.

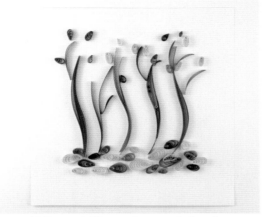

11 Add leaves of different colors onto the branches. Add some small loose coils between the trunks to serve as dew.

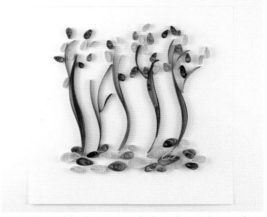

12 Keep adding leaves onto the branches. Make sure that the leaves are not too crowded, but in picturesque disorder.

13 Add some teardrop coils among the trunks to mimic falling leaves.

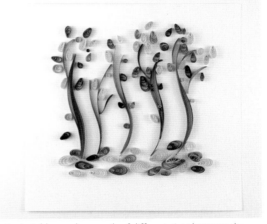

14 Add some loose coils of different sizes between the leaves, which will serve as dew.

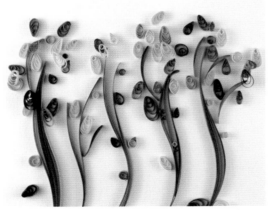

15 Pile a small number of leaves upon the leaves in the upper part of the picture to create a three-dimensional effect.

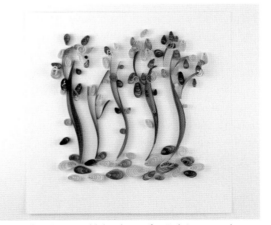

16 Continue to add dewdrops of varied sizes onto the leaves and branches. Complete the work by adjusting its contents and fixing with white latex.

18. Frost's Descent

Frost's Descent (*shuangjiang*), which normally falls on Oct. 23 to 24 each year, is the last solar term in autumn, meaning that winter will soon come. By then, it begins to become cold and dew turns into frost. Farmers start to plough the land and grow spring crops. Health care then becomes very important. According to some Chinese customs, on this day people should eat persimmons, which will help them keep out the cold and prevent illnesses.

This work presents this solar term with hairy crabs, a Chinese delicacy that has long enjoyed a good reputation. Hairy crabs are the most delicious during this time, as they have been storing nutrition in their bodies for an entire year and now begin to mate. The crab basket and several crabs in this work are the best interpretation of this solar term. The crab in the lower-right corner is making threatening gestures like a beast of prey, and the one in the upper-left corner is struggling out of the basket, showing strength and vitality. The three smaller crabs outside the basket enrich the whole picture and suggest that this is the mating season for hairy crabs. The whole work is ingenious in composition and full of vitality.

Crab basket: ⬤⬤⬤ coil: quadrangular coil; crescent: basic crescent

Big crabs: ⬤ coil: loose coil, bamboo-leaf coil, tight coil, irregular coil

Small crabs: ⬤ coil: loose coil, tight coil

Background: white watercolor paper (suggested size: 27 by 27 centimeters)

1 Make a six-layer crescent with the burnt-umber paper slips. Make several two-layer crescents of different lengths with the earth-yellow paper slips.

2 Make more than 20 single-layer paper coils with the earth-yellow and chocolate paper slips and pinch them into quadrilaterals consisting of straight lines.

3 Roll a dark-green paper slip from one end.

4 Roll up the whole slip to make a bigger loose coil. Fix it with white latex.

5 Gather the outer layers of the loose coil and make an angle out of it with both hands.

6 Make three more angles using the same method. Let the loose coil unroll naturally to get an irregular loose coil, which will serve as the body of the crab.

7 Make more than 10 loose coils with the dark-green paper slips and then pinch them into bamboo-leaf coils, which will serve as the crab's feet.

8 Make eight coils in the shape of comma with the dark-green paper slips to serve as the final sections of the crab's feet.

9 Make a loose coil with the dark-green paper slip. Use your thumb and forefinger to cave in one side to form the shape of the crab claw.

10 Use the same method to make one more crab's claw of slightly different size.

11 Make two tight coils with the dark-green paper slips and two coils in the shape of comma. Place the tight coils into the comma coils to serve as the eyes of the crab. Put together the different body parts of the crab.

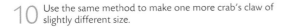

12 Make another big crab with the dark-green paper slips following steps 3 to 11.

13 Make three smaller crabs with the dark-red paper slips following the same method.

14 Place the burnt-umber crescent at the bottom of the picture, and then make the outline of the crab basket with the earth-yellow crescents, leaving an opening in the lower-right corner. Fix the outline with white latex.

15 Fill the earth-yellow and chocolate quadrilaterals into the outline.

16 Keep adding quadrilaterals, superimposing them atop the first layer of quadrilaterals.

17 Add the body and eyes of the big crab to the opening in the lower-right corner of the basket.

18 Add a pair of claws to the upper part of the crab, with the claw on the left grabbing the basket.

19 Add the feet to the right of the crab.

20 Add the second layer of feet on the first layer, making the feet overlap with each other. Be sure that each crab has a pair of claws and four pairs of feet.

21 Add four feet on the left side of the crab. The feet can overlap each other.

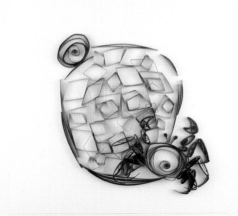

22 Add the body of the second hairy crab on the upper-left side of the basket.

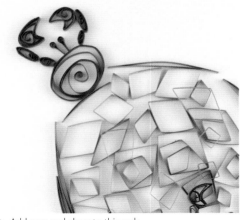

23 Add eyes and claws to this crab.

24 Add the first layer of feet to this crab.

25 Add the second layer of feet.

26 Add a small crab on the right side of the picture.

27 Add two small crabs to the lower-left corner of the picture. Complete the whole work by adjusting the contents and fixing with white latex.

19. Beginning of Winter

Beginning of Winter (*lidong*) normally falls on Nov. 7 to 8 each year. By that time, water has begun to ice, farmers have reaped their harvests and gotten them well-stored, and animals have hidden themselves underground for hibernation. In ancient China, on this day, the emperor would host a ceremony to greet the coming of winter and the ordinary people would also exchange greetings.

This work depicts the scene of "pheasants transforming into big clams," which is typical of Beginning of Winter. Legend has it that, after Beginning of Winter, bigger birds like pheasants disappear suddenly. However, on the seaside emerge big clams whose colors and designs resemble those of the pheasants. Therefore, Chinese people in ancient times considered that the pheasants had transformed themselves into clams. The mountains, river and pheasants in the picture give the viewers a sense of desolation.

Materials and Elements

Mountains: ●●●○ crescent: irregular crescent

Water: ○ line: broken line; loop: basic loop

Pheasants: ●● line: curved line; coil: tight coil, marquise coil

Background: white watercolor paper (suggested size: 27 by 27 centimeters), light-blue embossed paper (suggested size: 21 by 21 centimeters)

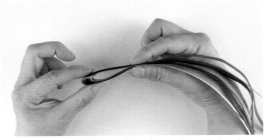

1 Paste the violet, Prussian-blue, deep-red and flesh color paper slips together at the beginning ends following the method of making a crescent. Fold it in half and then pull out different lengths of the slips from the tail end, leaving some space between the slips at the folding place. Pinch the folding place with your fingers to form an angle.

2 Move a small distance from the folding place to the tail end. Repeat step 1 and make the second angle.

3 Move still farther toward the tail end and make the third angle with the same method. Cut the redundant slips at the tail end and then fix the end with white latex to form an irregular crescent. This is the first peak.

4 Make two big and four smaller peaks of different patterns using the above method. The big peaks have three sharp angels each and the small peaks have two.

5 Make broken lines and basic loops with the flesh color paper slips to serve as river water.

6 Make three flying pheasants with the Prussian-blue and deep-red paper slips. Make the body with curved lines, the heads with tight coils, and the wings with marquise coils.

7 Arrange a piece of light-blue embossed paper in the center of the white watercolor paper. Place a big peak in the middle of the embossed paper.

8 Add the second big peak to the lower-right side of the central peak.

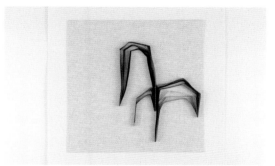

9 Add a small peak beneath the central peak.

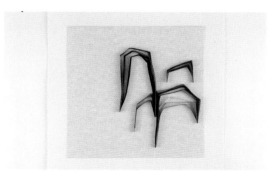

10 Add a small peak onto the top of the second big peak.

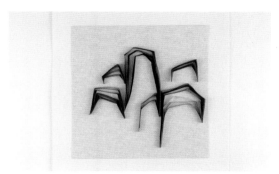

11 Add two small peaks to the left side of the big central peak, one upon the other.

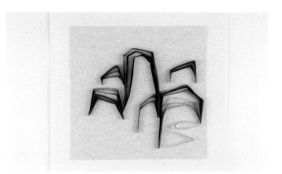

12 Add river water to the lower-right corner of the picture.

13 Add river water to the lower-left corner of the picture.

14 Add three pheasants in the sky. Complete the work by adjusting its contents and fixing with white latex.

20. Lesser Snow

Lesser Snow (*xiaoxue*) normally falls on Nov. 22 to 23 each year. By then, it has become cold and it may also snow in some places, though not heavily, and hence the name Lesser Snow. Everything on earth turn sluggish and lose vitality. Thus, the severe winter begins.

This work uses the white paper slips to display trees covered with snow. A leafless tree stands in the snow; two birds perch on a branch. Are they forgetting to migrate? How will they survive the ice and snow?

Materials and Elements

Tree trunk and branches: ⬤ crescent: basic crescent, raindrop crescent, S crescent, harp crescent; loop: leaf loop, raindrop loop, half-circle loop, irregular loop

Stone: ⬤ coil: irregular coil

Birds: ⬤⬤⬤ coil: teardrop coil, ring coil; line: broken line

Fog: ⬤⬤ coil: tight coil

Snowflakes: ⬤ coil: loose coil

Ground: ⬤ loop: irregular loop; crescent: basic crescent

Background: white watercolor paper (suggested size: 27 by 27 centimeters), violet embossed paper (suggested size: 21 by 21 centimeters)

1 Make some teardrop coils with the lake-blue paper slips to serve as the bodies and tails of the birds. Make some broken lines out of the orange-yellow paper slips to serve as the birds' beaks. Make two ring coils with the white paper slips to serve as the eyes of the birds.

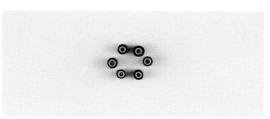

2 Make some tight coils with the light-blue and Prussian-blue paper slips, with the light-blue color inside and the Prussian-blue color outside. They will serve as the diffuse fog on the ground and create the atmosphere of a cold winter.

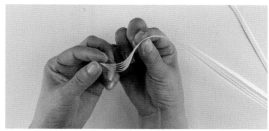

3 Put five white paper slips together. Treat one end the same way you make a basic crescent.

4 After a basic crescent is made, bend it towards the opposite direction so that it is encircled inside a raindrop loop.

5 Cut the redundant part and paste both ends with white latex. The raindrop crescent is complete.

6 Make more than 10 raindrop crescents of different sizes and layers.

7 Make some loops with the white paper slips. Then pinch them into leaf loops, raindrop loops, and half-circle loops and irregular loops.

8 Make more than 10 basic crescents, S crescents and harp crescents of different patterns with the white paper slips.

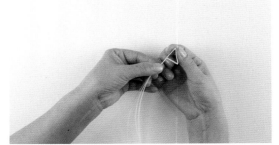

9 Now let's make a stone. Take out five white paper slips and paste them together at the beginning ends. Then fold them at 1 centimeter away from the beginning end.

10 Fold them again at 1.5 centimeters away from the first folding place.

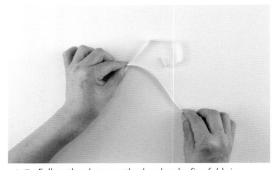

11 Fold them again at 2 centimeters away from the second folding place.

12 Follow the above method and make five folds in ascending distance.

13 Pull out different lengths of paper slips at tail ends.

14 Roll it into a triangle-shaped irregular coil just as you do to make a loose coil. Fix the tail end with white latex to serve as the stone.

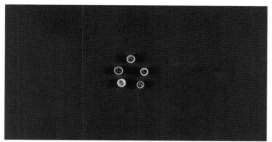

15 Make several loose coils with the white paper slips to serve as snowflakes.

16 Paste the violet embossed paper in the center of the white background paper. Arrange a basic crescent and an irregular loop at the bottom of the picture to serve as the ground.

17 Add a harp crescent as the tree trunk.

18 Add basic crescent branches and S crescent branches to the top of the trunk that bends towards right.

19 Continue to add crescent branches to form the main branches of the tree.

20 Add some crescents on the main branches to serve as forks.

21 Add two raindrop crescents on the ground in imitation of fallen branches.

22 Add some raindrop crescents to the branches.

23 Continue to add raindrop crescents between the branches to make the picture look fuller.

24 Add various types of loops on the ground in imitation of trees in the distance.

25 Add the stone to the bottom of the trunk.

26 Add loose coils between the branches in imitation of falling snowflakes.

27 Add blue tight coils here and there in the picture to create a foggy effect.

28 Finally, add two small birds that face each other onto the branch on the right. Complete the work by adjusting its contents and fixing with white latex.

21. Great Snow

Great Snow (*daxue*), which means heavy snow literally, normally falls on Dec. 6 to 8 each year. Different from Lesser Snow, Great Snow has a higher chance of snowing. And the snow is heavier, lasts longer and has a wider coverage. As a saying goes: "During Lesser Snow, the ground is covered with snow, but during Great Snow, the rivers are frozen all over." By this time, the weather is very cold, the rivers are covered with ice and snow, and the whole earth is dressed in white.

This work presents the solar term of Great Snow with the snow-swept grassland in China's northern Inner Mongolia. Two yurts stand lonely in the whirling snow, showing the boundlessness of nature. The white smoke rising from the chimneys of the yurts adds "human" taste, as well as warmth to the picture.

Materials and Elements

Main body of the yurts: ◯ ⬤ ⬤ crescent: basic crescent

Yurt doors: ⬤ crescent: basic crescent

Yurt chimneys: ⬤ ◯ coil: rectangular coil, teardrop coil; line: curved line

Decorative patterns on the yurts: ◯ crescent: spiral crescent

Small sand dunes: ⬤ crescent: basic crescent

Snowflakes: ◯ coil: loose coil

Background: white watercolor paper (suggested size: 27 by 27 centimeters), lake-blue embossed paper (suggested size: 21 by 21 centimeters)

1 Make three basic crescents of different sizes with the white paper slips to serve as the yurt's roof.

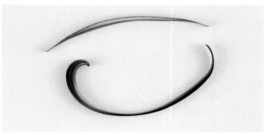

2 Make two long and thin basic crescents with the lake-blue and burnt-umber paper slips to serve as the top and bottom of the yurt.

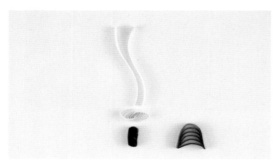

3 Make a basic crescent door and a rectangular coil chimney with the deep-red paper slips. Make a teardrop coil chimney and curved smoke with the white paper slips.

4 The component parts of a yurt are basically finished.

5 Follow the same method to make a smaller yurt.

6 Make more than 10 spiral crescents with the white paper slips to serve as the decorative patterns on the yurt.

7 Make six basic crescents with the Prussian-blue paper slips to serve as the small sand dunes.

8 Make many loose coils with the white paper slips to serve as snowflakes.

9 Paste the lake-blue embossed paper in the center of the white watercolor paper. Place the white and lake-blue crescents on the upper-right corner of the embossed paper to set up the top of the bigger yurt.

10 Fill the top of the yurt with two small white crescents.

11 Add the bottom and door to the yurt below the top.

12 Add a chimney to the top of the yurt.

13 Add a smaller yurt to the left of the bigger yurt. Add white smokes to the chimneys of the two yurts.

14 Add the white spiral crescents to the yurts as decorative patterns.

15 Add a small sand dune made of the Prussian-blue basic crescents to the lower-right corner of the picture.

16 Add another small sand dune to the lower-left corner of the picture.

17 Add snowflakes made of white loose coils above the yurts.

18 Cover the picture with snowflakes. Pay attention that the snowflakes are arranged in proper density.

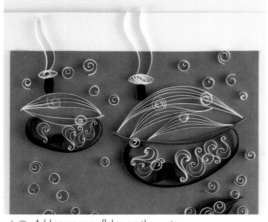

19 Add some snowflakes on the yurts.

20 Add snowflakes on the small dunes and complete the work by adjusting its contents and fixing with white latex.

22. Winter Solstice

Winter Solstice (*dongzhi*) normally falls on Dec. 21 to 23 each year. Like Summer Solstice, it is also one of the earliest confirmed solar terms. On that day, the sun's rays reach the southernmost end of the Earth and are almost directly over the Tropic of Capricorn. The daytime in the Northern Hemisphere is the shortest of the year. Before the Han Dynasty (202–220 BC), Winter Solstice was celebrated as the New Year. It was not until the time of Emperor Wu (156–87 BC) that Winter Solstice became a festival independent of the Spring Festival. Moreover, Winter Solstice is also a traditional date to offer sacrifices to heaven and ancestors. In ancient times, on this day, the emperors would host a grand ceremony to offer sacrifices to heaven while ordinary people would worship their ancestors.

Compared with other works in this book, this work adopts a more "realistic" method to make elements and present scenes. Every branch is made of multi-layered paper slips and thus looks thick and strong. It may seem to be a little bit "clumsy," but can still be considered a unique mode of representation and creation. The pale-looking and leafless branches reveal the harshness of winter and the withering of all things on earth. The twigs are in a jumble, but they show the vitality hidden in the tree trunk, which might burst out at any time through the tender buds. This tree makes us feel the alternation between *yin* and *yang*.

Materials and Elements

Stones: ● coil: half-circle coil, marquise coil

Tree trunk: ○ ● line: curved line

Branches and twigs: ○ line: curved line

Snow: ○ coil: marquise coil, loose coil

Background: white watercolor paper (suggested size: 27 by 27 centimeters), light-blue embossed paper (suggested size: 21 by 21 centimeters)

1 Make two half-circle coils with the ultramarine-blue paper slips.

2 Put the two half-circles together and wrap them with a layer of paper slip with the same color in imitation of a stone.

3 Make several stones of different sizes and shapes with the half-circle coils and marquise coils. The shape can be more various with the appropriate transformation of these elements.

4 Take out some white and burnt-umber paper slips. Fold them in half and paste more layers of paper slips onto it to make a thick tree trunk. Pay attention that the white and burnt-umber paper slips are arranged in good intervals to produce a hierarchical effect.

5 Superimpose white paper slips and make some curved lines of varied lengths to serve as tree branches.

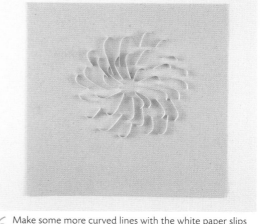

6 Make some more curved lines with the white paper slips to serve as thinner twigs.

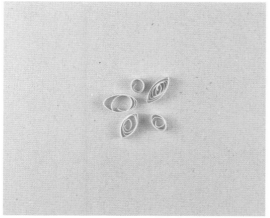

7 Make several marquise coils and loose coils of varied sizes and shapes with the white paper slips to serve as snow on the ground.

8 Paste the light-blue embossed paper onto the center of the white background paper, and then pave the ultramarine-blue stones at the bottom of the picture.

9 Add white marquise coils between the stones as white snow.

10 Add the vertical tree trunk on the stone.

11 Add some thicker white branches on the top and the right side of the trunk. The branches on the top are generally U-shaped.

12 Add thicker white branches on the left side of the tree trunk.

13 Add thinner twigs onto the trunk and branches in the upper half of the picture.

14 Add twigs onto the branches on the left side of the trunk.

15 Add some twigs also onto the branches on the right side. To help it look more natural, avoid making the twigs on both sides symmetrical.

16 Finally, add some more twigs to the gaps between branches to create a luxuriant effect. Complete the work by adjusting its contents and fixing with white latex.

23. Slight Cold

Slight Cold (*xiaohan*) normally falls on Jan. 5 to 7 each year, meaning the weather is cold, but yet not the coldest. However, in China, it is often colder in Slight Cold than in Great Cold, and the former is the coldest of all the 24 solar terms. Therefore, Sight Cold really symbolizes the advent of severe cold.

    This work uses daffodils to present this solar term. A cluster of daffodils in a small porcelain pot with some pebbles beneath is a common scene in many Chinese families. Using green paper slips for the stem, white and yellow paper slips for the flowers, interspersed with dark-colored pebbles, the author has rendered the elegant and pure daffodils perfectly.

Materials and Elements

Daffodil petals: ◯ coil: teardrop coil

Daffodil stamens: ⬤◯ coil: tight coil, ring coil

Daffodil stems: ◯◯◯◯◯◯ crescent: S crescent

Pebbles: ⬤⬤⬤⬤⬤⬤◯◯ coil: loose coil, teardrop coil

Background: white watercolor paper (suggested size: 27 by 27 centimeters), cobalt-blue embossed paper (suggested size: 21 by 21 centimeters)

1 Make more than 10 S crescents of assorted sizes and patterns with six layers of paper slips arranged from light to dark green, which will serve as the stems of the daffodils.

2 Make four teardrop coils with the white paper slips to serve as four flower petals. Put them together to form a daffodil.

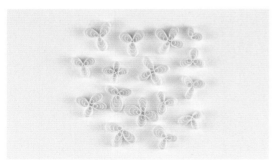

3 Make more than 10 daffodils, some with four petals, some three or two.

4 Make some tight coils with the orange-red paper slips. Wrap them with medium-yellow ring coils, which will serve as the stamens of the daffodils.

5 Make more than 20 teardrop coils of different sizes and shapes to serve as pebbles with paper slips in various shades of brown, gray and flesh color.

6 Make several more loose coils to serve as pebbles with paper slips of the colors shown in the picture. This is to enrich the composition of the pebbles.

7 Paste the cobalt-blue embossed paper onto the center of the white watercolor paper.

8 Place teardrop coil pebbles at the bottom of the picture.

9 Continue to pile up pebbles of various colors.

10 Add loose coil pebbles between the teardrop coil pebbles.

11 Add several longer daffodil stems above the pebbles. Pay attention that these stems face different directions so that they look more natural.

12 Add shorter stems between the longer ones.

13 Pile up more stems to create a luxuriant and three-dimensional effect.

14 Add daffodil flowers above the stems.

15 Continue to add flowers to create a luxuriant and leafy effect.

16 Decorate the flowers with yellow stamens. Complete the work by adjusting its contents and fixing with white latex.

24. Great Cold

Great Cold (*dahan*) means the weather is extremely cold. It is the last of the 24 solar terms in a year falling normally on Jan. 20 to 21 each year. By then, it is very cold and the ground is frozen and everything on earth has dried up. However, after a whole year's hard work, the Chinese begin to prepare for the coming new year's celebration, the Spring Festival, the most important festival of the Chinese people. Therefore, this period is cold but filled with festival joy and happiness.

Instead of depicting the severe cold in winter, this work, quite unexpectedly, resorts to warm colors to display this solar term. The medium-yellow background, supplemented by two strings of red peppers, shows the flourishing scene of the Chinese people celebrating the new year in cold. Meanwhile, the peppers, like firecrackers being set off in the Spring Festival, look delightfully attractive.

Red peppers: crescent: cicada-wing crescent

Background: white watercolor paper (suggested size: 27 by 27 centimeters), medium-yellow embossed paper (suggested size: 21 by 21 centimeters)

1 Put five dark-red and four deep-red paper slips together, with the dark-red ones above and deep-red ones below. Paste them together at the beginning end and then roll up the beginning end with a slotted tool.

2 Follow the method of making crescents. Hold the beginning end with one hand, and pull out different lengths of paper slips with another hand, so the paper slips have different radians.

3 Cut the redundant paper slips and paste together the tail end. Wrap the tail end with the beginning end and fix with white latex. This element is a variation of the crescent.

4 Hold the beginning and tail ends at where they meet with one hand, and pinch the other side to form a sharp angle.

5 As the element thus made resembles the cicada's wing, we name it cicada-wing crescent, which embodies the flexibility of Chinese paper quilling. You can also give full play to your imagination in the making process and create some unique elements.

6 Make many cicada-wing crescents of different sizes and layers with the deep-red and dark-red paper slips, which will be used as red peppers.

7 Make some cicada-wing crescents of different sizes and shapes with the vermilion paper slips.

8 Paste the medium-yellow embossed paper onto the center of the white background paper.

9 Add the first double-color cicada-wing crescent to the upper left of the picture. Add two deep-red cicada-wing crescents on its right as the red peppers on the top.

10 Add some cicada-wing crescents of assorted colors below the red peppers on the right side.

11 Add some cicada-wing crescents blow the red peppers on the left side.

12 Continue to add red peppers on the lower part of the picture. The two strings of red peppers can be arranged more casually for a natural effect.

13 Add red peppers to the ends of the strings, making the strings look wide at top and narrow at bottom.

14 Add smaller red peppers here and there in the picture so that the strings look denser and fuller. Complete the work by adjusting its contents and fixing with white latex.

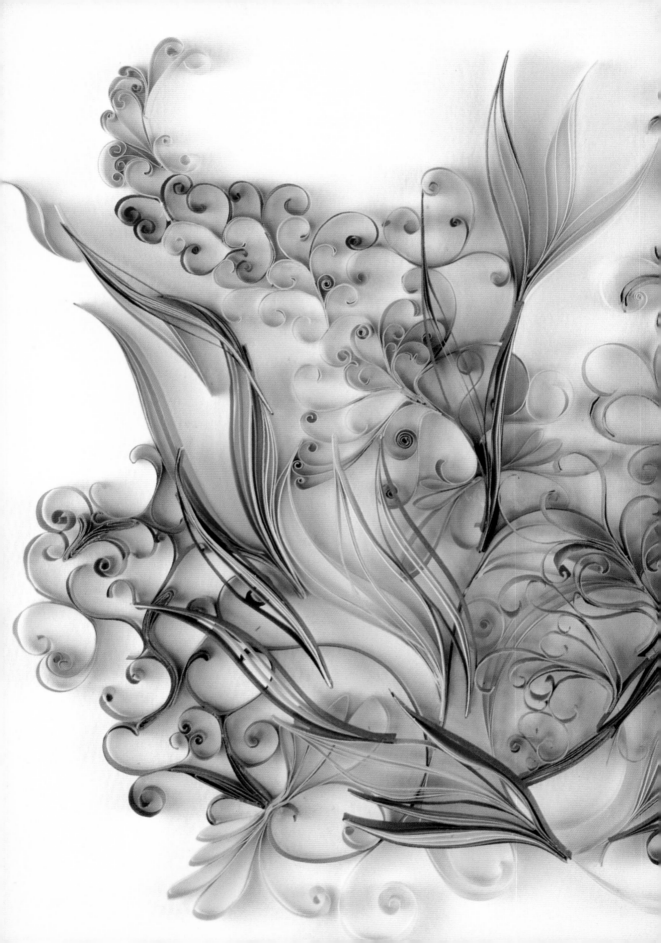

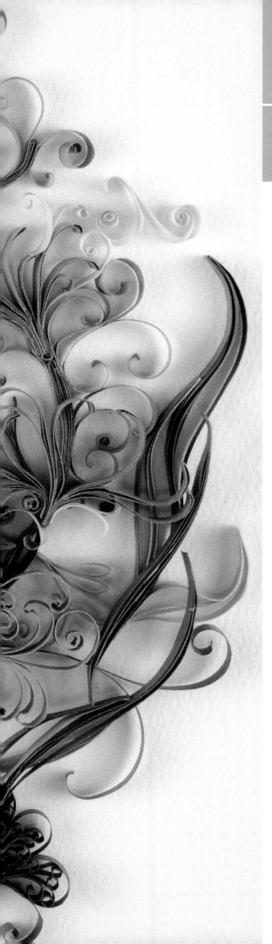

CHAPTER IV
Intermediate Tutorial

*I*n the previous chapter, we learned how to combine basic elements to express a theme by creating some simple works of paper quilling. In this chapter, we focus on depicting scenes and still life in all seasons. The works require a more flexible use of elements and a better command of color coordination, as the compositions are more complicated. You are encouraged to give full play to your own creativity and imagination and try to create your own representation of the four seasons based on the examples offered here.

Fig. 26 *Flowers and Grass*
Dimensions: 39 by 39 centimeters
Using many long-tail scrolls to make the petals, this work is rather creative in composition.

1. Spring in the Air

In this work, the author uses Chinese-style paper quilling to represent flowers
and birds, which are common themes in traditional Chinese paintings. Flower-
and-bird paintings focus on depicting flowers, birds, fishes and insects and are an
important part of Chinese painting. The author adopts the freehand brushwork
and fine brushwork techniques to present flower leaves and birds respectively.
The pink flower sits in the green leaves, with a blue bird perching on the branch.
The whole work displays a beautiful scene in spring.

Materials and Elements

Bird's outline: ● ● ●   crescent: basic crescent

Big feathers: ● ●   loop: raindrop loop

Small feathers: ○   coil: tight coil

Bird's tail: ● ●   loop: basic loop

Feathers on bird's head: ● ● ○ ○ ●   line: curved line; coil: teardrop coil, tower coil

Bird's eye: ● ○   coli: tight coil

Bird's beak: ●   coil: tower coil

Leaves: ○ ● ● ●   crescent: basic crescent

Flower petals: ● ● ● ● ● ○   crescent: basic crescent, irregular crescent; loop: irregular raindrop loop

Stamens: ○ ○   coil: tight coil, basic coil

Background: white watercolor paper (suggested size: 39 by 54 centimeters)

1   Make three basic crescents with cobalt-blue, sky-blue and orange-red paper slips as the outline of the bird. Make three basic loops with cobalt-blue and sky-blue paper slips in descending size as the tail of the bird.

2   Make a group of curved lines in ascending length with cobalt-blue, sky-blue and white paper slips. Paste them together at the beginning end to serve as the feathers on the bird's crest. Make a teardrop coil with the flesh-color paper slip and a tower coil with the lemon-yellow paper slip, which serve as the feathers on the bird's face. Make a tight coil with the black and lemon-yellow paper slips as the eye of the bird. Make another tower coil with the black paper slip as the beak.

3   Make more than 20 raindrop loops with the cobalt-blue and sky-blue paper slips as the big feathers on the bird's body.

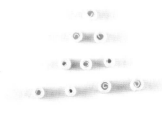

4   Make 10 tight coils with the white paper slips as the smaller feathers.

5 Make a large number of crescents of different sizes and layers as leaves with the paper slips in various shades of green and light gray. The crescents may vary slightly in shape.

6 Wrap lemon-yellow tight coils with pink-green basic coils in the shape of comma to make stamens. Make more than 10 stamens.

7 Make four basic crescents of different sizes and layers with the paper slips in various shades of pink and flesh color, which will serve as the first petal type.

8 Make seven basic crescents with the paper slips in various shades of pink and flesh color. Pinch them into irregular shapes, which will be the second petal type.

9 Make nine raindrop loops with the paper slips in various shades of pink and flesh color. Use the pinching and pasting techniques to create the shapes in the picture, which will serve as the third petal type.

10 Add three irregular raindrop loop petals onto the lower right of the picture.

11 Keeping adding irregular raindrop loop petals and crescent petals to form the basic form of the flower.

12 Add some irregular crescents around the flower to make it look fuller.

13 Add stamens in the center of the petals.

14 Add some green crescents below the flower as green leaves.

15 Continue to add leaves on the right side of the picture around the flower.

16 Continue to add green leaves to the upper right of the flower.

17 Continue to add green leaves to the lower left of the flower.

18 Add a group of green leaves to the upper right of the picture, keeping some distance from the green leaves below it.

19 Add a group of green leaves to the upper left of the flower.

20 Add some smaller crescents between the green leaves to make them look more luxuriant.

21 Add some smaller irregular crescent petals here and there between the green leaves.

22 Add the outline of the bird made of crescents to the upper left of the flower.

23 Add the tail to the bottom of the outline.

24 Add the eye and the beak.

25 Add feathers on the crest and the face.

26 Fill the outline with bigger feathers made of raindrop loops.

27 Add smaller feathers made of tight coils to the gaps between the big feathers. Complete the work by adjusting its contents and fixing with white latex.

2. Verdant Mountains and Blue Water

Mountains and rivers are important themes in traditional Chinese paintings that focus on depicting the natural mountain scenes. In this work, the author delineates a beautiful scene of verdant mountains and blue water in summer borrowing the blank-leaving techniques commonly adopted in Chinese landscape paintings, thus rendering the work transparent and vast.

Materials and Elements

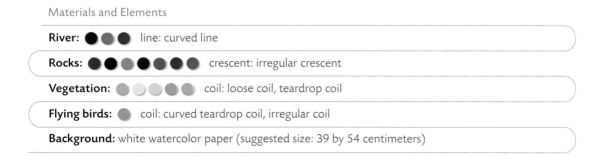

River: ●●● line: curved line

Rocks: ●●●●●●● crescent: irregular crescent

Vegetation: ●●●●●● coil: loose coil, teardrop coil

Flying birds: ● coil: curved teardrop coil, irregular coil

Background: white watercolor paper (suggested size: 39 by 54 centimeters)

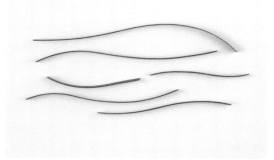

1 Take out six burnt-umber paper slips and five lake-blue paper slips. Paste their beginning ends and tail ends together with white latex. Then bend them into the shape of a river. Fix the slips at appropriate places with white latex.

2 Make six olive-green curved lines of varied lengths as the ripples on the river.

3 Make a multi-layered basic crescent with olive-green, deep-gray, chocolate, and brown-gray paper slips.

4 Pinch the basic crescent into the shape of an irregular rock crescent.

5 Use the same method to make more than 10 rock-shaped irregular crescents of different sizes, layers and patterns with the olive-green, dark-green, purple-red, burnt-umber, chocolate, brown-gray and deep-gray paper slips.

6 Make six crescents of varied sizes and shapes with the chocolate and burnt-umber paper slips to serve as another pattern of mountain rocks.

7 Make a large number of loose coils to serve as vegetation with pink, pale-pinkish-gray, pink-green, and gray-green paper slips.

8 Make the shape of a flying bird with a curved teardrop coil and two comma-shaped irregular coils with the light-gray paper slips. Follow the same method to make five flying birds.

9 Make eight teardrop coils of different sizes with the yellow-green paper slips to serve as another form of vegetation.

10 Arrange the burnt-umber and lake-blue curved lines at the bottom of the picture in imitation of a river.

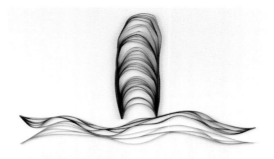

11 Put the biggest rock element in the center of the picture.

12 Add a smaller rock element in the blank below the big rock element to form a complete peak.

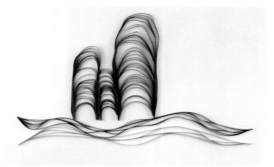

13 Add the second peak on the left side of the first peak.

14 Add another slightly bigger peak on the left side of the second peak.

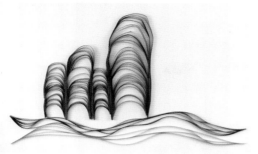

15 Add another smaller peak on the left side of the third peak.

16 Add a smaller peak on the right side of the first peak.

17 Add the last peak on the right side.

18 Arrange the rock crescents into the blank space below the peaks.

19 Fill in the blank space in the river with olive-green curved lines to enrich the changes of the river.

20 Add yellow-green teardrop coils to the bottom of the peaks as vegetation on the mountains.

21 Continue to add some loose coils in imitation of colorful vegetation. The loose coils can be piled up on the top to create a three-dimensional effect.

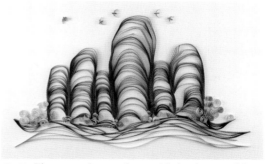

22 Pile up more loose coils to enrich the picture and then add five flying birds to the upper part of the picture. Complete the work by adjusting its contents and fixing with white latex.

3. Blossoming Moth Orchids

With smooth lines and a concise shape, this work depicts blooming moth orchids in spring. Unlike most of the works in this book that depend on the collocation of various elements for formation, this work relies more on the plasticity of paper slips, using many curved lines to outline the leaves of the moth orchids. The inside of the leaves is also filled with different kinds of curved lines. The stems and flowers, on the other hand, consist of regular elements. The combination of such curved elements exhibits a more flexible technique of creation, rendering the work richer.

Materials and Elements

Leaves: ●○ line: curved line

Stems: ○ crescent: basic crescent

Petals: ○○●● coil: irregular teardrop coil

Background: white watercolor paper (suggested size: 40 by 40 centimeters)

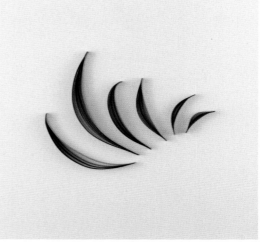

1 Make five single-layered teardrop coils with a paper slip in various shades of pink. Wrap them with another paper slip and fix it with white latex to serve as petals of the moth orchids. You may refer to the method of making lotus leaves in "Limit of Heat" (page 90). Follow this method and make more than 20 petals, with each petal consisting of a different number of teardrop coils.

2 Make several basic crescents of different sizes and layers as the stems of the orchid with the light-green paper slips.

3 Paste five light-green paper slips together at the beginning end, cut the tail end into slips of different lengths, and scrape each slip until it bends, thus forming a group of curved lines. Make a large number of curved line groups of different layers, sizes and radians to serve as leaf veins.

4 Make the outlines of two big leaves growing toward the right at the bottom of the picture with the dark-green paper slips.

5 Make the outlines of two leaves growing toward the left above the bigger leaves.

6 Make the outlines of several leaves with the dark-green paper slips.

7 Continue to make the outlines of the leaves with curved lines made from the dark-green paper slips.

8 Arrange the light-green curved line groups completed in step 3 into the leftmost leaves in imitation of leaf veins.

9 Continue to add light-green veins into the leaves at the bottom.

10 Add light-green veins into the middle leaves.

11 Finally, add light-green veins into the leaves on top. The leaves are complete.

12 Add light-green basic crescents above the leaves as the stems of the moth orchids.

13 Add two flowers to the upper left of the picture, each consisting of several petals.

14 Add two flowers on the upper right of the picture.

15 Add some more petals to the blank space in the picture to increase the hierarchical effect. Complete the work by adjusting its contents and fixing with white latex.

4. Swan on Water

In summer, the sky is clear, the water is blue and everything on earth is in its prime of life. This work displays exactly such a scene in summer, vigorous and prosperous. The author uses blue as the main color to present river water and the swan, making viewers feel nice and cool. She uses curved lines in varied shades of blue as ripples, which look agile and rhythmic. The swan, which consists of crescents, is full of charm, braving the waves with obvious ease. Together, the waves and the swan constitute a beautiful and vivid summer scene.

Materials and Elements

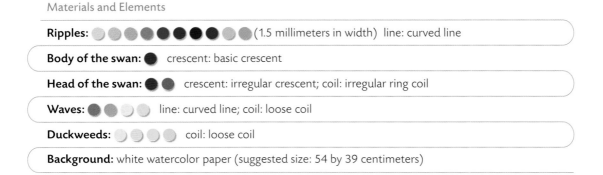

Ripples: ⚪⚪⚪⚫⚫⚫⚫⚫⚪⚪ (1.5 millimeters in width) line: curved line

Body of the swan: ⚫   crescent: basic crescent

Head of the swan: ⚫⚫   crescent: irregular crescent; coil: irregular ring coil

Waves: ⚫⚫⚪⚪   line: curved line; coil: loose coil

Duckweeds: ⚪⚪⚪⚪   coil: loose coil

Background: white watercolor paper (suggested size: 54 by 39 centimeters)

1 Paste together a large number of paper slips in varied shades of blue (mainly Prussian blue and ultramarine blue) that are 1.5 millimeters in width at their beginning ends. Make them into the shape of ripples by bending and pinching.

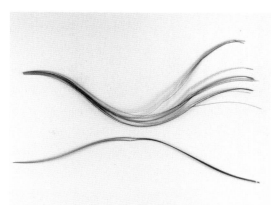

2 Make two groups of curved lines with paper slips in different shades of medium blue with cobalt blue as the main color. They will serve as ripples.

3 Make two groups of ripples with paper slips in varied shades of light blue with sky blue as the main color.

4 Cut the Prussian-blue paper slips and make them wide at one end and narrow at the other (similar to the cutting method in "Rain Water," on page 48). Make five bigger basic crescents with these paper slips. They will be used to make the neck, wing and stomach of the swan.

5 Make a basic crescent with the Prussian-blue paper slip. Change its form by pinching and use it as the head of the swan. Make a ring coil with the rose-red paper slip and pinch it into the shape of a crest on top of the swan's head.

6 Make some curved lines with cobalt-blue paper slips, which will serve as surging waves.

7 Make a large number of basic crescents of varied sizes with the Prussian-blue paper slips, which will serve as the feathers on the stomach and tail of the swan.

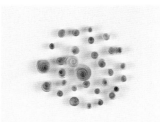

8 Make many loose coils with paper slips in different shades of light blue, which will serve as waves.

9 Make some loose coils with the flesh-color, lemon-yellow, medium-yellow and light-green paper slips, which will serve as duckweeds.

10 Add deep-blue ripples at the bottom of the picture. Adjust and make them natural and smooth in shape.

11 Stack a group of medium-blue ripples on the first group of ripples.

12 Add another group of medium-blue ripples above the first group of ripples.

13 Add two groups of waves in shades of light blue on both sides of the picture. Add two Prussian-blue crescents on top of the waves to form the swan's stomach.

14 Add the crescent wing and neck to the swan.

15 Add feathers onto the swan's body .

16 Keep adding feathers onto the swan. Pay attention to the direction of the feathers.

17 Add feather onto the swan's tail hierarchically.

18 Add the head and red crest to the swan.

19 Add surging cobalt-blue waves to the left side of the ripples.

20 Add loose coils in shades of light blue between the ripples to represent waves.

21 Add some light-blue waves above the water as well.

22 Add flesh-colored, lemon-yellow and medium-yellow loose coils here and there in imitation of duckweeds.

23 Add light-green loose coils to the ripples on the right side of the picture to represent green duckweeds. Complete the work by adjusting its contents and fixing with white latex.

5. A Fine Autumn Day

This work displays an autumnal scene. Between the undulating hills stand trees of various kinds, their leaves either becoming yellow or still emerald green. Above the hills are the blue sky with white clouds floating leisurely. On the left side of the picture is a tall tree, serving as the focus of the whole work.

Overall, the picture looks clean and neat, a fine embodiment of the theme of a beautiful autumn. The author uses loops to make different kinds of trees. In making the bigger tree, she has changed the loop shapes with the freehand style, a traditional Chinese painting technique. The free and unrestrained style, we believe, will enlighten viewers in creation.

Materials and Elements

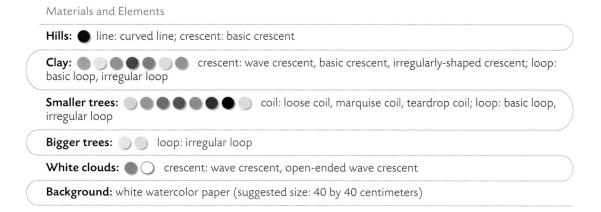

Hills: ● line: curved line; crescent: basic crescent

Clay: ●●●●●●● crescent: wave crescent, basic crescent, irregularly-shaped crescent; loop: basic loop, irregular loop

Smaller trees: ●●●●●●●●● coil: loose coil, marquise coil, teardrop coil; loop: basic loop, irregular loop

Bigger trees: ●● loop: irregular loop

White clouds: ●○ crescent: wave crescent, open-ended wave crescent

Background: white watercolor paper (suggested size: 40 by 40 centimeters)

1 Make several wave crescents that are open at the tail with the white and gray paper slips.

2 Make more than 10 wave crescents of different sizes and layers with the white paper slips.

3 Make more than 10 loose coils and marquise coils with the green shades and lemon-yellow paper slips.

4 Make a large number of teardrop coils with the green shades and lemon-yellow paper slips.

5 Make a basic loop with four lemon-yellow paper slips first, then work out some irregular sharp angles on it.

6 Make more than 10 irregular loops with the light-green and lemon-yellow paper slips, some double-colored and some single-colored.

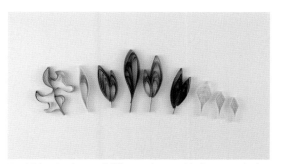

7 Make nine loops of different shapes with the green shades, lemon-yellow, and burnt-umber paper slips. Use different techniques to vary the loop shapes.

8 Make nine wave crescents of different sizes and layers with the warm-gray, light-green, sky-blue and chocolate paper slips.

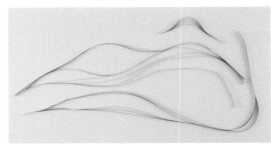

9 Make some crescents and loops of varied shapes with the warm-gray, purple-red, lemon-yellow and orange-yellow paper slips.

10 Make a crescent with the brown-gray paper slips and two multi-layer curved lines with both ends pasted together. The middle part of the lines can be pasted together naturally.

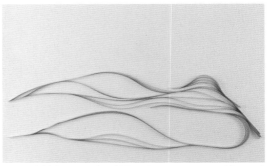

11 Add the first multi-layer brown-gray curved line to the lower part of the picture. The line can be arranged freely.

12 Add the second multi-layer brown-gray curved line and wave crescent to form undulating hills.

13 Add some loops as clay between the hills.

14 Keep adding wave crescents between the hills as clay.

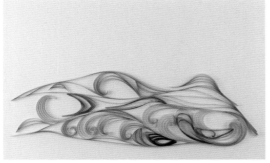

15 Add some more wave crescents and loops between the hills.

16 Add a row of light-green raindrop loops to the gap between the hills on the left side of the picture.

17 Add two rows of deep-green trees to the other two gaps between the hills.

18 Add loops of different colors to the hills as trees. The loops can be superimposed to create a three-dimensional effect.

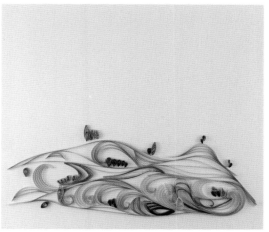

19 Add coils of assorted colors as trees at the top of the hills.

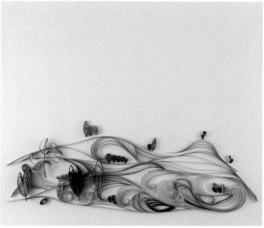

20 Superimpose some bigger loops as trees in the vicinity of the hills' left side.

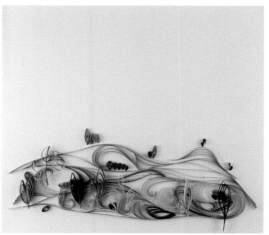

21 Superimpose some irregular loops on the right side of the hills as trees closer to the foreground.

22 Add several irregularly shaped double-colored loops to the upper-left side of the hills.

23 Keep adding single-colored irregular loops to form the overall skeleton of a big tree.

24 Add some irregular loops onto the big tree.

25 Add some green loose coils between the hills.

26 Work out the first group of white clouds on the right side of the big tree with wave crescents and a section of the open-ended wave crescents.

27 Work out the second group of white clouds on the upper right of the picture with wave crescents.

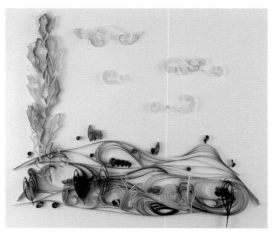

28 Add several smaller wave crescents as white clouds. Complete the work by adjusting the contents of the picture and fixing with white latex.

6. Flower Petals Falling in Profusion

"Flower petals falling in profusion" recreates the artistic conception created by a Chinese idiom derived from a classical Chinese essay written by Tao Yuanming (376–427) of Eastern Jin Dynasty (317–420). This work is an effort to reduplicate this dynamically beautiful scene: The spring wind brings down the flowers from the trees and makes them float and drift in the woods. The elements used in this work, large in number, are all evolved from the basic elements of Chinese-style paper quilling. Unrestrained and flexible, they embody the freedom in creating works of Chinese-style paper quilling.

Materials and Elements

Flowers: loop: irregular raindrop loops

Trees: crescent: irregular crescent; loop: basic loop, raindrop loop, half-circle loop

Background: white watercolor paper (suggested size: 40 by 40 centimeters)

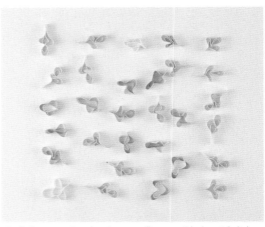

1 Make a two-layer raindrop loop with a pink and a white paper slip. Work on it with your hand until it takes on the shape in the picture. This will serve as the flower.

2 Follow step 1 and make more flowers with the pink, light-pink, white and pink-purple paper slips.

3 Make a large number of basic loops, raindrop loops, and half-circle loops with the white and black paper slips to form the forest.

4 Make many loops with the blue shades, violet, deep-red paper slips to from the forest. These loops can be made into different shapes as you like.

5 Make many basic crescents with the blue shades, violet and deep red paper slips. Work on them with your hands until a sharp angle appears in the center of each crescent. They will serve as the forest.

6 Add several irregularly-shaped crescents at the bottom in the middle of the picture.

7 Keep adding irregularly-shaped crescents to the right and left sides.

8 Add blue loops to the middle of the crescents.

9 Keep adding smaller blue loops.

10 Put some blue irregularly-shaped crescents on the first layer to create a three-dimensional forest.

11 Add more blue loops.

12 Arrange black loops inside the blue irregularly-shaped crescents.

13 Arrange white loops of various kinds inside the irregularly-shaped blue crescents.

14 Add some white loops beneath the forest.

15 Add more white loops to the forest.

16 Add flowers to the upper left of the forest. Arrange the flowers in the shape of an arc, as if they were swaying in the breeze.

17 Arrange many more flowers on the upper right of the forest.

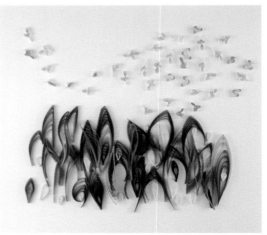

18 Complete the work by adjusting the contents of the picture and fixing with white latex.

7. Fruits of All Seasons

This work depicts fruits of all seasons with paper slips of assorted colors. The appropriate use of elements, the color scheme and the ingenious structural layout make the yellow lemons, purple grapes, scarlet cherries, red apples and green oranges stand out on the paper. The whole work, realistic and vivid, looks exactly like a still life oil painting.

Materials and Elements

Fruit container: ⚪⚪⚪⚪⚪⚫⚫ line: curved line; crescent: basic crescent

Grapes: ⚫⚫⚫ coil: loose coil

Lemons: ⚪⚪ loop: irregular raindrop loop

Cherries: ⚫⚫⚫ crescent: irregular crescent; coil: irregular coil

Oranges: ⚪⚪⚪⚪⚫ crescent: irregular crescent

Apples: ⚪⚫ crescent: irregular crescent; coil: irregular coil

Background: white watercolor paper (suggested size: 54 by 39 centimeters)

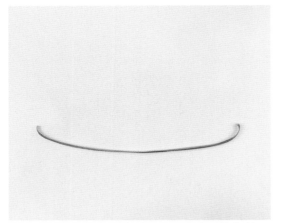

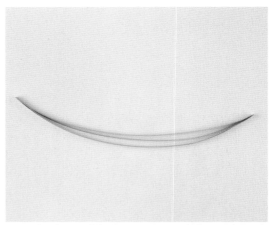

1 Take out several paper slips in various shades of light blue. Paste together their beginning ends and tail ends. Scrape it until it becomes a circular arc.

2 Make a long and thin basic crescent with three pink-purple paper slips.

3 Make a large number of loose coils to serve as grapes with paper slips in various shades of purple.

4 Make two 20-layer raindrop loops with the lemon-yellow and medium-yellow paper slips. Pinch them into the shape of a lemon.

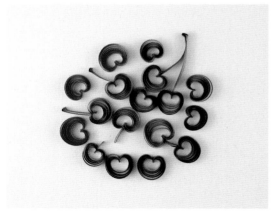

5 Make more than 10 basic crescents with the rose-red, magenta, and purple-red paper slips. Paste together both ends of the crescents to serve as cherries. Bend the slips to make the cherry stalks.

6 Follow the method of making cherries to make seven oranges with the paper slips in various shades of green.

7 With the same method, make two apples and apple stalk with the scarlet and pink paper slips supplemented with the technique of pinching.

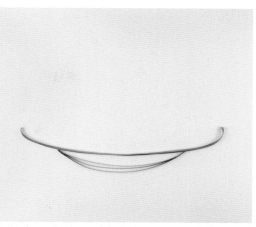

8 Work out the shape of the fruit container at the bottom of the picture.

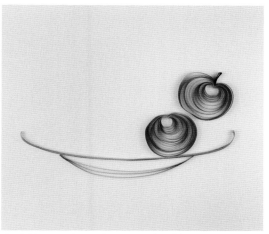

9 Add two apples on the upper right of the container.

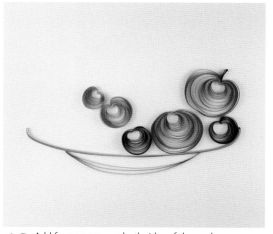

10 Add four oranges on both sides of the apples.

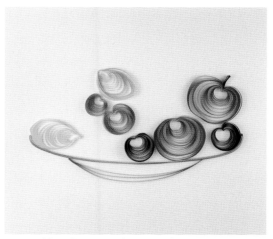

11 Add two lemons on the upper left of the container.

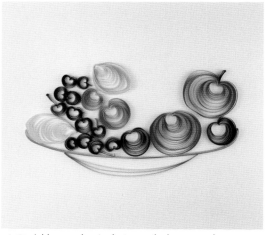

12 Add some cherries between the lemons and oranges.

13 Add some grapes between the oranges and apples.

14 Arrange three oranges upon the apples and oranges to create a three-dimensional effect.

15 Arrange some grapes upon grapes to mimic grapes in a string.

16 Similarly, arrange some cherries upon the first layer of cherries.

17 Finally, add two cherries on the lower-left side of the container to make the picture complete.

18 Finish the work by adjusting its contents and fixing with white latex.

8. Flowers of All Seasons

This work produces flowers of all seasons through the comprehensive use of different elements. The flowers, including lotus flowers, peach flowers, roses, chrysanthemums, daisies, canna flowers, scarlet sages and moth orchids, are blossoming and compete for glamour, giving the viewer a sense of prosperity and affluence. The vine basket in the shape of a crescent gathers the slightly disorganized flowers, making the picture in good order and complete.

Materials and Elements

Basket: ● ● ● line: broken line; crescent: wave crescent, basic crescent

Lotus flowers: ◐ loop: irregular raindrop loop; crescent: basic crescent

Moth orchid petals: ◐ ● ○ coil: irregular teardrop coil

Orchids: ○ ○ ● crescent: basic crescent

Daisy: ○ ○ ● ● crescent: irregular crescent; coil: tight coil

Peach flower: ● ◐ coil: tight coil, teardrop coil

Roses: ● ◐ ○ coil: loose coil, irregular coil

Scarlet sages: ● crescent: *ruyi* scepter-shaped crescent

Canna flower: ⬤ crescent: wave crescent

Chrysanthemum: ◯ ⬤ crescent: *ruyi* scepter-shaped crescent

Scattered petals: ◯ ◑ loop: raindrop loop

Leaf Type I: ◯ ◔ ⬤ ◑ ◔ ◑ crescent: wave crescent

Leaf Type II: ◯ ⬤ crescent: irregular crescent

Leaf Type III: ◯ ◯ ⬤ loop: basic loop

Leaf Type IV: ⬤ ◑ coil: teardrop coil

Background: white watercolor paper (suggested size: 54 by 39 centimeters)

1 Make a broken line with one chocolate paper slip, one
deep-gray paper slip and one brown-gray paper slip.
Put together four longer chocolate paper slips and make a
wave crescent on each end. Fold the paper slips in the middle
sections as shown in the picture, which will serve as the handle
of the flower basket.

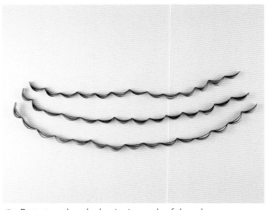

2 Paste together the beginning ends of three longer
chocolate paper slips. Make more than 10 basic crescent
elements along it, fixing the crescents by pasting. Make three
such elements to serve as the flower basket.

3 Make a raindrop loop with three pink paper slips. Pinch
the top of the loop until a sharp angle appears. Fix the
angle by pasting it with white latex to produce a lotus bud.
Make another raindrop loop with the same method. Add two
pink basic crescents on both sides of the loop to produce a
blooming lotus flower.

4 Make more than 10 moth orchid petals of different
sizes with the pink, rose-red and flesh-color paper slips
following the method of making moth orchids in "Blossoming
Moth Orchids" (page 144).

5 Make six basic crescents of different shapes and sizes with the pale-pinkish-gray and light-pink paper slips to serve as the orchid petals. Make some crescents to serve as leaves with the olive-green paper slips.

6 Make a crescent with one lemon-yellow, one grass-green and one olive-green paper slip. Fold the crescent in half from the middle part. Fix both ends of the crescent with white latex to form a heart shape. Use the same method to make a smaller heart with the lemon-yellow and light-yellow paper slips and place it into the first heart to form a daisy petal. Make six such petals and paste them around the tight coil made of the lemon-yellow and grass-green paper slips to form a complete daisy.

7 Make six teardrop coils with the cameo-brown paper slips and paste them around the tight coil made of the scarlet paper slips to form a peach flower.

8 Superimpose a white paper slip and a light-pink paper slip and make them into a loose coil as the stamen. Make some single-layered teardrop coils and paste them around the stamen.

9 Make more single-layered white teardrop coils and paste them around the stamen.

10 After all the light-pink and white teardrop coils are pasted around the stamen, pinch it into an irregular shape.

11 Sort out the work to complete a rose. Make another rose with the rose-red paper slips using the same method.

12 Make many smaller *ruyi* scepter-shaped crescents with the deep-red paper slips and paste them into four strings as shown in the picture. They are scarlet sages.

13 Make several wave crescents with the scarlet paper slips as the components of the canna flowers.

14 Make some *ruyi* scepter-shaped crescents with the medium-yellow and pink-purple paper slips to serve as chrysanthemum petals.

15 Make some raindrop loops with the medium-yellow and orange-red paper slips to serve as scattered petals.

16 Make more than 10 wave crescents of different sizes to serve as Leaf Type I with the lemon-yellow, grass-green, olive-green, pink, lake-blue and pink-purple paper slips.

17 Make three *ruyi* scepter-shaped crescents with the medium-yellow and olive-green paper slips. Then paste their tail ends onto the sharp angles at the beginning ends to serve as Leaf Type II.

18 Make three basic loops with the lemon-yellow, pale-pinkish-gray, and olive-green paper slips. Then arrange them into a bigger olive-green basic loop hierarchically to form Leaf Type III.

19 Make some teardrop coils with the dark-green and olive-green paper slips to serve as Leaf Type IV.

20 Arrange three groups of continuous crescents at the bottom of the picture as the bottom of the flower basket.

21 Add the broken line elements and the double-head wave crescents, which will serve as the handle of the basket.

22 Add chrysanthemum petals into the right side of the basket.

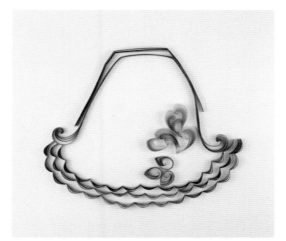

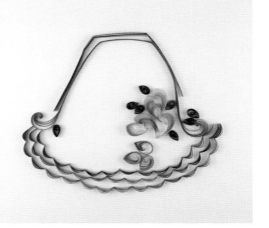

23 Add the second type of leaves below the chrysanthemum petals.

24 Add the fourth type of leaves around the chrysanthemum petals.

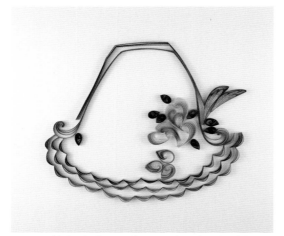

25 Add the third type of leaves to the right side of the basket.

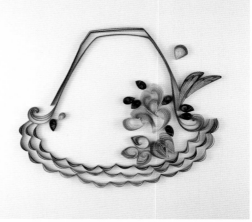

26 Add some scattered petals to the blank space inside and outside the basket.

27 Arrange the scarlet sages on the left side of the basket.

28 Put together and superimpose the components of the canna flowers and then arrange them in the left side of the basket.

29 Add the first type of leaves around the inside of the basket.

30 Add crescent leaves in and outside of the basket.

31 Arrange two roses inside the basket.

32 Arrange a peach flower on the right side of the basket.

33 Add moth orchid petals here and there in the basket.

34 Arrange a daisy upon the peach flower.

35 Add two lotus flowers.

36 Finally, superimpose the orchids at the bottom of the left side of the basket. Complete the work by adjusting its contents and fixing with white latex.

CHAPTER V
Advanced Tutorial

*B*y now, you should have become an expert in paper quilling. What you need to do is to observe and experience life carefully, give the fullest play to your own creativity and imagination, and then create works of your own style with paper slips. The four works in this chapter take spring, summer, autumn and winter as the theme, using details to express the artist's own impression of the seasons and his emotion. They display the artist's skills in the Chinese artistic techniques and his strong personal style in artistic creation. The works are hierarchically rich and use many graceful curved lines to create artistic conceptions that are either far-reaching, tranquil, open-minded or statically beautiful, and the overall style is impressionist, natural and smooth. Are you ready for a try? Then start right now!

Fig. 27 *Chrysanthemums*
Dimensions: 27 by 27 centimeters
Chrysanthemums are referred to as hermits of flowers metaphorically. They are much loved by ancient Chinese men of letters. The author depicts full-blown chrysanthemums in autumn with bright colors, changing their aloof and cold image into enthusiastic beauty.

1. Spring Mountains

As the warm spring breeze melts ice and snow and turns trees green, the mountains also become a riot of colors, full of life and vitality. In this work, the author depicts the colorful mountain rocks and trees with paper slips of assorted colors.

Mountain rocks: ●●○●●●○○●● crescent: irregular crescent; line: broken line

Trees: ●● crescent: *ruyi* scepter-shaped crescent, irregular crescent

Bushes: ○◐○●●●●●●○○○○●●● coil: loose coil, teardrop coil

Background: white watercolor paper (suggested size: 39 by 54 centimeters)

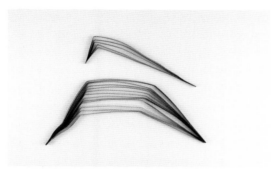

1 Make two basic crescents with the ultramarine-blue paper slips. Then shape them as shown in the picture by pinching. They will serve as the upper part of the first group of rocks.

2 Superimpose the flesh-color, earth-yellow and light-brown paper slips and make a basic crescent with them. Then make two basic crescents, one bigger and the other smaller, with the dark-green paper slips. Pinch the three basic crescents into the shapes shown in the picture, which will serve as the lower part of the first group of mountains.

3 Make two crescent elements as shown in the picture with chocolate and burnt-umber paper slips, which will serve as the lower part of the second group of rocks.

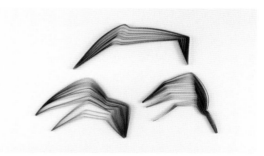

4 Continue to make the upper part of the second group of rocks with the chocolate, burnt-umber and medium-gray paper slips.

5 Make two irregular crescents with the medium-gray, light-brown and flesh-color paper slips, which will serve as the third group of rocks.

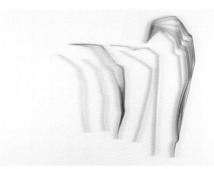

6 Make an irregular crescent with the light-green paper slips. Then make several sections of broken lines with the light-purple paper slips. They will serve as the fourth group of rocks.

7 Make the fifth group of rocks as shown in the picture with the ultramarine-blue paper slips.

8 Make more than 10 *ruyi* scepter-shaped crescents with deep-green paper slips, which will serve as trees. Make some *ruyi* scepter-shaped crescents with the grass-green paper slips. Pinch some of them into irregular shapes.

9 Make more than 20 teardrop coils with paper slips of different shades of green as the main color, which will serve as bushes.

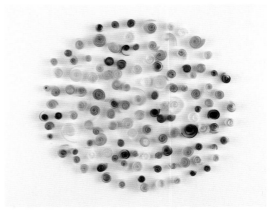

10 Make many loose coils with paper slips with different shades of green as the main colors, which will serve as another type of bushes.

11 Add the upper half of the first group of rocks to the lower-right corner of the picture. Add the lower half of the first group of rocks.

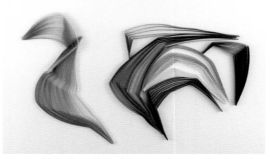

12 Add the lower half of the second group of rocks to the lower-left corner of the picture.

13 Keep adding the upper half of the second group of rocks.

14 Add the third group of rocks to the upper-left corner of the picture.

15 Add the light-green outline of the fourth group of rocks to the right side of the third group of rocks.

16 Arrange the light-purple curved lines into the fourth group of rocks as fillers.

17 Add the two bigger elements in the fifth group of rocks to the upper-right corner of the picture.

18 Add the three smaller elements to the lower-right corner of the fifth group of rocks.

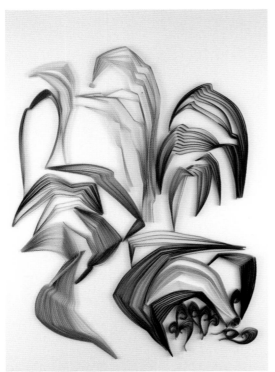

19 Add deep-green *ruyi* scepter-shaped crescents to the bottom of the first group of rocks to form trees.

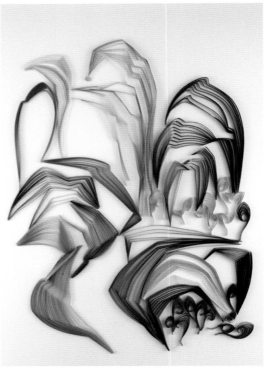

20 Add deep-green and grass-green trees under the fifth group of rocks.

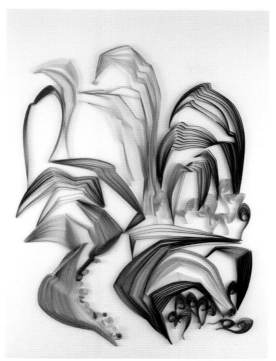

21 Add loose coils and teardrop coils along the right side of the lower half of the second group of rocks in imitation of bushes.

22 Add bushes to the left side of the second group of rocks as well.

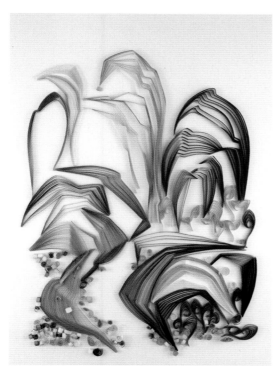

23 Add bushes here and there among the first group of rocks.

24 Add some bushes to other groups of rocks, too. Complete the work by adjusting its contents and fixing with white latex.

2. Summer Water

In mid-summer, the sunshine nourishes all things on earth and there is life and vitality everywhere. During this time, the best way for families to escape from the summer heat is to go to the seaside and play in the water. In this work, the author chooses the scene of people surfing in the sea. The huge surging waves and the small lone surfers form a vivid visual contrast, showing that, although man is in awe of nature, he also tends to challenge it.

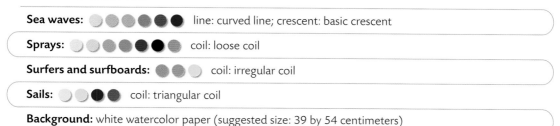

Materials and Elements

Sea waves: ⚪⚪⚪⚪⚪⚫⚫ line: curved line; crescent: basic crescent

Sprays: ⚪⚪⚪⚪⚫⚫⚪ coil: loose coil

Surfers and surfboards: ⚫⚫⚪ coil: irregular coil

Sails: ⚪⚪⚫⚫ coil: triangular coil

Background: white watercolor paper (suggested size: 39 by 54 centimeters)

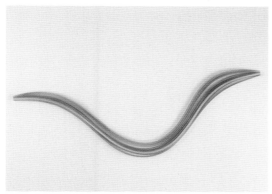

1 Take out a large number of paper slips in shades of light blue, paste them together on both ends, and bend them as shown in the picture.

2 Make two groups of crescents with lake-blue, cobalt-blue and violet paper slips.

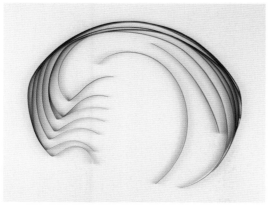

3 Make some curved lines as shown in the picture with dark-blue and violet paper slips.

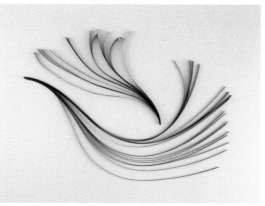

4 Make two groups of curved lines by scraping the ultramarine-blue and peacock-blue paper slips.

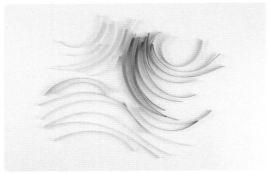

5 Make many curved lines of different lengths with the light-blue, violet and light-green paper slips.

6 Make a lot of loose coils with paper slips in shades of blue and dark-green and light-purple paper slips.

7 Make two surfers with earth-yellow coils. Make two surfboards with orange-yellow and lemon-yellow paper slips.

8 Make five triangular coils with light-green, lemon-yellow, violet and cobalt-blue paper slips, which will serve as sails.

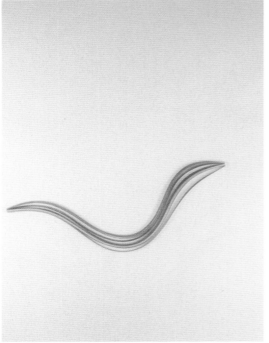

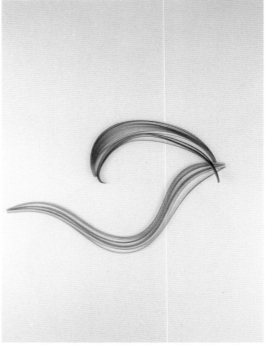

9 Add the group of curved lines made from paper slips in shades of light blue to the center of the picture in imitation of the sea level.

10 Add crescent sea waves above the sea level.

11 Surround the crescent waves with a ring of curved lines made of the deep-blue and violet paper slips to create waves that are turning up.

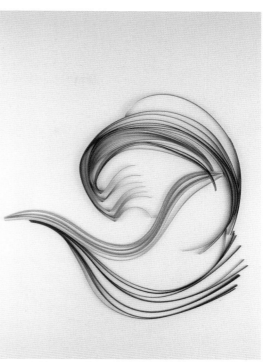

12 Add groups of curved lines made from the ultramarine-blue and peacock-blue paper slips below the sea level to create a three-dimensional effect.

13 Add one more group of ultramarine-blue curved lines.

14 Add some curved lines at the bottom of the surging sea waves in imitation of waves surging forward.

15 Add some curved lines to the sea level and the upper-left corner of the picture.

16 Add some curved lines above the surging sea waves.

17 Add many loose coils at the bottom of the picture to represent splashing water.

18 Add a large number of loose coils above the sea level.

19 Keep adding loose coils on the top of the picture. Be sure the color of the loose coils gradually fades from the bottom to the top of the picture.

20 Add the two surfers on the surging sea waves.

21 Add sails between the sea waves on the top of the picture.

22 Complete the work by adjusting its contents and fixing with white latex.

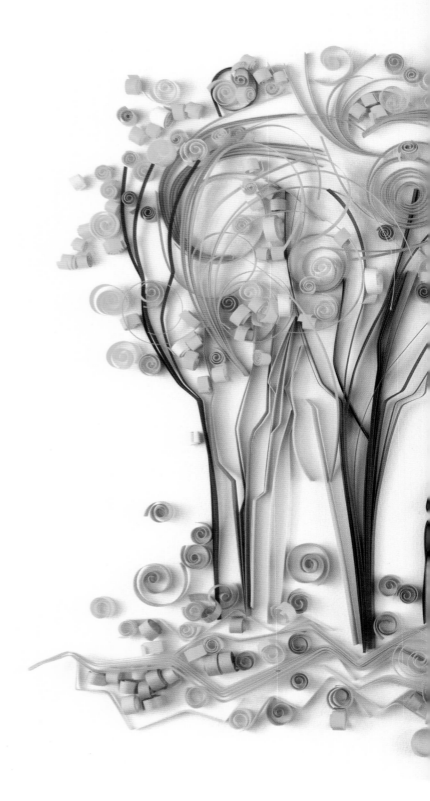

3. Autumn Forest

Autumn is the season for harvesting. It is also when things begin to wither and turn from prosperity to decline. This work depicts autumn leaves turning yellow and falling gracefully down to the ground. The artist uses broken and curved lines to create trees and loose coils for leaves, with two spotted deer as decorations. The whole work is natural, smooth and lively, showing the beauty of harmony in nature.

Materials and Elements

Soil: ⚪⚪⚪ line: broken line

Trees: ⚫⚫⚪⚫ line: broken line

Tree crowns: ⚫⚫⚫ line: curved line

Leaves: ⚪⚪⚪⚪⚪ coil: loose coil

Deers: ⚫⚫⚫⚫⚫⚫ coil: irregular coil, loose coil

Background: white watercolor paper (suggested size: 54 by 39 centimeters)

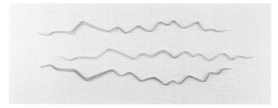

1 Take out a large number of lemon-yellow, light-yellow, and medium-yellow paper slips, paste them together on both ends with white latex, and fold them into three groups of broken lines.

2 Make nine broken lines with the light-yellow and lemon-yellow paper slips.

3 Paste purple-red paper slips together at the beginning ends and make six groups of broken lines as shown in the picture, which will serve as trees.

4 Make many broken lines with the light pink-purple, white and light-gray paper slips.

5 Take out some orange-yellow and orange-red paper slips, paste them together at the beginning ends, and scrape them into six groups of curved lines. These will serve as the crowns of the trees.

6 Make more than 10 spiral curved lines with the orange-red and deep-red paper slips.

7 Make many loose coils with flesh-color paper slips and paper slips in shades of yellow, which will serve as tree leaves and patterns on deers.

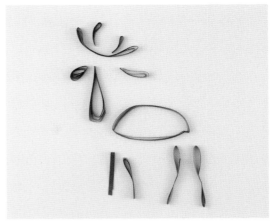

8 Make coils with the burnt-umber paper slips. Pinch them into different body parts of the first deer.

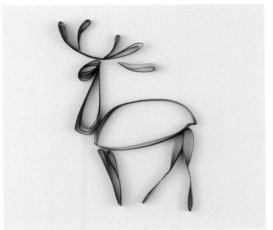

9 Piece together the body parts to form the first deer.

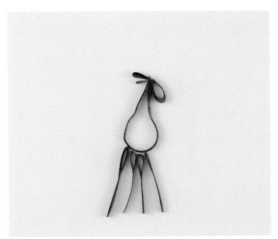

10 Make the second deer with the same method.

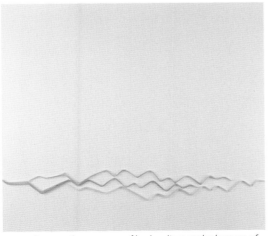

11 Arrange three groups of broken lines at the bottom of the picture to serve as soil.

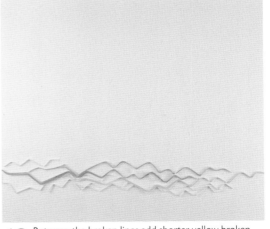

12 Between the broken lines add shorter yellow broken lines.

13 Add three groups of purple-red broken lines on the soil to form two trees. The left tree is composed of two groups of broken lines superimposed upon each other.

14 Add the remaining three groups of purple-red broken lines.

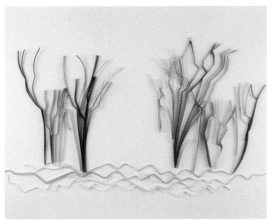

15 Add pink-purple, white and light-gray broken lines between the purple-red trees to create the impression of many trees.

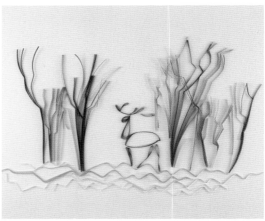

16 Add the first deer between the trees.

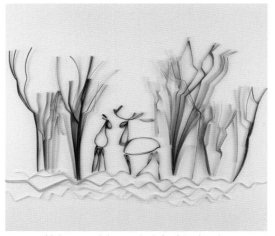

17 Add the second deer to the left of the first deer.

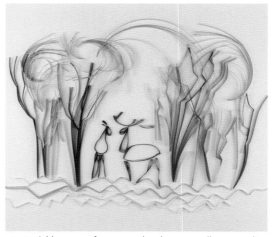

18 Add groups of orange-red and orange-yellow curved lines above the tree trunks as the crowns of the trees.

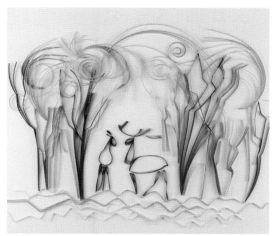

19 Arrange some orange-yellow spiral curved lines on the crowns.

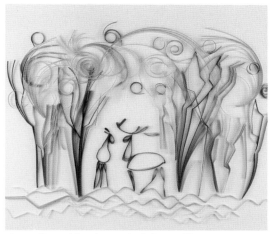

20 Keep adding deep-red spiral curved lines.

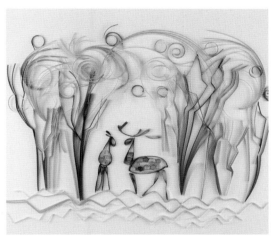

21 Add loose coils in shades of yellow on the body of the deers for their spotted coats.

22 Arrange many loose coils in shades of yellow and flesh color on the soil to represent fallen leaves.

23 Add a large number of loose coils in shades of yellow and flesh color onto the crowns in imitation of tree leaves. Pay attention to be sure the leaves on the trees are brighter in color than the fallen leaves.

24 Add some falling leaves between trees. Complete the work by adjusting its contents and fixing with white latex.

4. Winter Snow

In winter, the freezing
northern wind brings heavy
snow, turning the earth into
a pure white world. In this
work, the artist presents
the theme of winter by
depicting a pair of foxes
hunting for food outside, a
frozen river, a vast expanse
of cold-resistant pines, and
snowflakes floating all over
the sky. The whole picture
is complete in composition,
vivid in shape, simple
but elegant in color, and
displays the beauty of
winter in northern China.

Materials and Elements

Foxes: ⚫⚪⚫ crescent: basic crescent, irregular crescent; coil: triangular coil, ring coil, marquise coil, irregular coil; line: curved line

River: ⚪⚪⚪ crescent: basic crescent, harp crescent

Pines: ⚫⚫⚫⚫⚫ line: curved line

Stones: ⚫⚫ coil: marquise coil

Snowflakes: ⚫⚪ coil: loose coil, curved teardrop coil, irregular coil

Snow: ⚪⚪⚪⚪⚪ coil: loose coil

Background: white watercolor paper (suggested size: 54 by 39 centimeters)

1 Make the red fox with the scarlet and burnt-umber paper slips. The body, limbs, and tails are made of crescents, the thorax and abdomen with curved lines, the head with irregular coil, the pattern on head with marquise coil and ring coil, the ears with triangular coils, and the eyes and the nose with long and slim ring coils.

2 Make the body parts of the yellow fox with the medium-yellow and burnt-umber paper slips following the same method used to make the red fox. Mind the changes on its face and limbs.

3 Piece together the different body parts of the red fox.

4 Piece together the different body parts of the yellow fox.

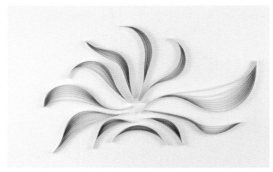

5 Make some basic crescents and harp crescents with the pink-blue paper slips. Make more crescents with paper slips in shades of light blue.

6 Make many groups of curved lines with paper slips in shades of purple and light-gray paper slips that are 1.5 millimeters and 3 millimeters wide.

7 Make some marquis coils with the medium-gray and green-gray paper slips to serve as the stones on the riversides.

8 Make some curved teardrop coils and loose coils with the pink-blue and white paper slips. Combine them to make snowflakes.

9 Make some snowflakes consisting of six diamond-shaped coils with the pink-blue and white paper slips.

10 Make a large number of loose coils with paper slips in shades of light blue.

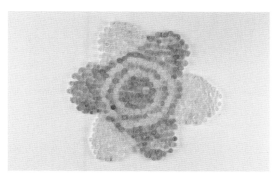

11 Make a great deal of loose coils with the light pink-purple and white paper slips.

12 Add the two foxes to the picture. Arrange some blue crescents under their feet to form the river.

13 Add more blue crescents to increase the river's three-dimensional quality.

14 Make two pines with groups of purple curved lines and arrange them above the foxes.

15 Continue to make four smaller pines to form a pine forest.

16 Add the gray marquise coils on the riversides to serve as stones.

17 Add a large number of pink-purple and white loose coils at the bottom of the picture to represent accumulated snow.

18 Add many pink-purple and white loose coils on the top of the picture in imitation of falling snow. Add some blue loose coils here and there in the picture to make the work richer in color.

19 Add snowflakes on the pine trees.

20 Add some snowflakes here and there in the picture. Complete the work by adjusting its contents and fixing with white latex.